GCSE (9-1) in Religious Studies

REVISION GUIDE

Level 1/Level 2
Beliefs in action from a Christian perspective

PEARSON EDEXCEL B (1RB0)

Brian Poxon

GCSE Religious Studies Pearson Edexcel B (1RB0) REVISION GUIDE

Level 1/Level 2 Beliefs in action from a Christian perspective

GCSE Religious Studies Pearson Edexcel B specifications and past exam questions © Pearson Education. References are included from the Oxford English Dictionary, some meanings are omitted, changed slightly or added to. Bible quotes refer to the New International Version.

ISBN: 978-1-78484-102-7 (pbk)

ISBN: 978-1-78484-118-8 (hbk)

ISBN: 978-1-78484-119-5 (ebk)

ISBN: 978-1-78484-155-3 (kin)

Published in the United Kingdom by PushMe Press.

www.pushmepress.com

Introduction

The purpose of studying for a GCSE in Religious Studies is twofold:

Firstly, it introduces a whole range of thinking about various issues that concern us all. These religious approaches are based on the collective learning of billions of people over thousands of years. They have been responsible for much of the greatest architecture and art ever produced, and their traditions have helped countless people gain a sense of identity and helped them to answer all sorts of questions about the meaning of and how they should live their lives best.

However, no religious tradition is without fault and great suffering has been caused in the name of the religions studied. To this day they provide direction about how people should live that has a profound effect upon how we live in our society. Both the good and bad found in religion are worthy of exploring and questioning, so that each individual can make up their own mind about a wide range of issues such as relationships, medicine, life and death, and war.

Secondly, in order to be successful in the exam, you build up a series of very useful skills such as listening, presenting, thinking, reading and writing as well as learning to work collaboratively and independently. These are transferable skills, which means that you can use them in other subjects and, more importantly, they are skills that you can use as a part of your continued learning when you leave school.

Good luck with your studying.

How to use this book

Students studying the Edexcel GCSE Religious Studies choose two religions to study. This revision guide focuses on Christianity, and a further revision guide covers Islam.

In this guide, detailed summaries are provided on each of the **THREE AREAS OF STUDY**, **FROM WHICH STUDENTS CHOOSE ONE** for Christianity and a different one for another religion to qualify for the Full Course GCSE. In the following guide, material is given on Christianity in Area of Study 1, Religion and Ethics; Area of Study 2, Religion, Peace and Conflict; and Area of Study 3, Religion, Philosophy and Social Justice. Each Area of Study has a 1 hour 45 minute examination, meaning students take two examinations at the end of the course, both worth 50% of the qualification. The exam section at the end of this guide gives a full breakdown of how the examination works

This book provides you with detailed summaries of all parts of the Pearson Edexcel B specification from the Christian perspective, as well as chapters on exam preparation and detailed advice on how to answer each type of question. It is organised according to the specification so that you can find topics easily.

We have put extra resources on our website which you can access by scanning the code at the end of the chapter with your smartphone, or you can enter the i-pu.sh code into your browser. The website resources are also organised under the specification headings. The code will take you directly to the module you have scanned and you can browse between modules on the site. You will find Key Quotes, Practice Questions and more. If you are reading a Kindle version of this book, you can click on the link at the end of each chapter.

At the beginning of each chapter, you will find a list of key words and their definitions. Many of these key words are in **BOLD** in the text so that you can see them used in context. In places, other words are highlighted as prompts for you to remember the content.

The last two chapters focus on preparing for the exam and how to answer the questions. You will find further advice on the website.

Contents

Religion & Ethics

Matters of Life and Death...*71*

Religion, Peace & Conflict

Crime & Punishment...*109*

Religion, Philosophy & Social Justice

Exam Success

Religion & Ethics

(1RB0/Area of Study 1)

Beliefs

Marriage & the Family

Living the Christian Life

Matters of Life & Death

Beliefs

KEYWORDS

- **ASCENSION** - Jesus being taken up to heaven forty days after his resurrection

- **ATONEMENT** - Being made right with God

- **AUTHORITY** - Having power to give guidance, commands and direction

- **BIBLE** - Christian holy book or Scriptures, made up of the Old and New Testaments

- **CREATION** - The process of how something came into existence

- **ESCHATOLOGY** - The study of the end of the world or "end times"

- **ETERNAL** - Lasting forever; having no beginning or end; outside of time

- **EVIL** - Wicked, morally wrong, bad: natural evil caused by nature; moral evil caused by human action

- **FORGIVENESS** - To grant pardon for an offence or sin

- **HEAVEN** - Spiritual realm thought to be the abode of God; the good afterlife

- **HELL** - Spiritual realm of punishment or the absence of God; the bad afterlife

- **IMMORTAL** - Living forever, never dying or decaying

- **INCARNATION** - Taking human form; God taking human form in Jesus

- **NICENE CREED** - An important statement of Christian belief originating in AD325 and still stated in Christian churches today

- **OMNIBENEVOLENT** - All loving

- **OMNIPOTENT** - All powerful

- **OMNIPRESENT** - Present everywhere

- **OMNISCIENT** - All knowing

- **ORIGINAL SIN** - The belief that humans are born with sin because of Adam and Eve's original disobedience to God

- **PASSION** - The last days of Jesus' life, including his suffering

- **RESURRECTION** - Jesus rising from the dead; overcoming death

- **SACRAMENT** - An event or ceremony where God's grace is received

- **SALVATION** - Deliverance from sin

- **SIN** - Anything that goes against God's law

- **SOUL** - The spiritual, non-physical and immortal part of a human

- **STEWARDSHIP** - To look after something that has been entrusted to your care

- **SUFFERING** - Undergoing pain, distress or hardship

- **TRINITY** - God the Father, Son and Holy Spirit

THE TRINITY

It is important to stress that Christians do not believe in three Gods, but one God shown in three equal ways, or three Persons. The Nicene Creed states that Christians **BELIEVE IN ONE GOD**, known as God the Father, God the Son and God the Holy Spirit. This is known as The Trinity.

- **THE FATHER** - In the Nicene Creed, God the Father is described as Almighty, and the Maker of everything, including the universe, heaven and earth. Roman Catholics believe that the Father is outside of time - eternal. Protestants believe God is everlasting inside of time. The word Father combines both the idea of authority and care, which is important for Christians when they worship God because they believe God is Almighty and All Loving at the same time.

- **THE SON** - In the Nicene Creed Jesus is described as the "only-begotten Son of God, eternally begotten" (eternally begotten mean Jesus has, like God, always existed and is unique, rather than the idea of God giving birth to Jesus). Jesus is both Divine (God) and human. He lived on earth and showed people how God wants them to live, suffered and died to forgive sins and was resurrected to show that God has the power to rise from the dead. Christians believe Jesus will judge all people on Judgement Day. In worship, Christians will often joyfully express their thanks to Jesus for being willing to suffer and give his life for them to "save them", and enable them to be forgiven.

- **THE HOLY SPIRIT** - After Jesus rose from the dead, he said that the Holy Spirit would come to give people guidance, and live with and in them as God's continuing presence on earth. The Nicene Creed describes the Holy Spirit as the "Lord and Giver of Life". The Holy Spirit gives comfort, peace and help, and inspires and guides Christians as they try to put beliefs into action. Christians believe that the Holy Spirit is omnipresent and by the Holy Spirit, God is with people today, enabling them to have a relationship with Him.

The Trinity is very important in Christian worship. Christians believe that the Holy Spirit helps them to have a relationship with God the Father as the Holy Spirit is God's presence on earth. That relationship with the Father is possible because God the Son has died to forgive sins and therefore broken down the barrier between God and humanity.

In **CHARISMATIC CHURCHES**, emphasis in worship is for a personal experience of God, and it is believed that a person can be "filled with the Holy Spirit". Charismatic services often stress that people can receive the "gifts of the Holy Spirit" such as healing and a language known as "tongues" to help communicate more closely with God.

Even though the word **TRINITY** is not mentioned in the Bible, The Trinity working as Three Persons in Unity can be seen in New Testament passages such as Matthew, Chapter 3 verses 13-17. As Jesus is baptised, the Holy Spirit comes to Him, and, at the same time, the Father speaks. Later in Matthew's Gospel, Jesus told his disciples to baptise people in the name of **THE FATHER**, **THE SON** and **THE HOLY SPIRIT**.

THE CREATION AND HUMANITY

Christians believe that God created the entire universe. The creation of the earth and humanity is outlined in **GENESIS** Chapters 1-3. The word Genesis means **BEGINNINGS**, and many Christians believe God created the universe "out of nothing" (**EX NIHILO**).

Genesis Chapter 1, one of two creation accounts, says that the creation took place over 6 days, starting with heavens, earth, light and darkness (day 1), sky and water (day 2), land, seas and vegetation (day 3), sun, moon and stars (day 4), fish and birds (day 5), land animals and humans (day 6). Uniquely, humans are created **IN THE IMAGE OF GOD**, which makes them capable of having a relationship with God, and they are given responsibility to "rule over" the earth.

- **CREATIONISM** - Some Christians take this story literally, and believe God created the world in six 24-hour days. This belief is called Creationism. Creationists do not accept the scientific view of the universe developing over billions of years after the Big Bang.

- **BIG BANG** - Other Christians believe that the creation story is not supposed to be factually accurate, but interpreted metaphorically. They would accept that God created the earth, but that could have been through the Big Bang, with evolution being the process through which life on earth developed.

Christians believe that the Trinity existed before the universe and was involved in its creation. God the Father commands the universe to exist through his word. John Chapter 1 verse 1 describes Jesus as God's Word, and in John 1:3 that God the Father created all things through God the Son, his word. In Genesis 1, The Holy Spirit is also described as present and "hovering over the waters", and many Christians see the Holy Spirit as the breath of God which gives life to everything.

Genesis 3 describes how after the earth and humans were formed, God and Adam and Eve had a perfect relationship until Adam and Eve chose to disobey God. This introduced sin into the world, and is known as The Fall. See Salvation section for more on this.

The Creation story is very important to Christians today because:

- **OMNIPOTENT** - It says that God is Omnipotent and that the world was planned by and is important to God

- **PURPOSE** - The world has a purpose and that nature and all life should be respected and cared for

- **UNIQUE** - Humans are unlike any other creatures as the creation story says that only humans were "breathed into" by God, giving them a soul. This means they have a vital role to fulfil their responsibilities which comes from them being made in the image of God. This care for the world on God's behalf is known as stewardship.

- **RELATIONSHIP** - Christians believe that, uniquely, humanity can have a relationship with God

THE INCARNATION

The word incarnation refers to a person who embodies a God or Deity. Christians believe that Jesus is God in human form. He is both fully God and fully human at the same time. The Old Testament says that a Messiah or deliverer would come to save or "rescue" humanity. Jesus is the Messiah who was incarnated - literally **TOOK ON FLESH** - to live on earth, teaching and showing people how God wants them to live.

Jesus was born to Mary after she was made pregnant through the Holy Spirt, and he lived a fully human life. Jesus ate, slept, felt pain and joy and this is very important to Christians as it means God knows what our human experience is like.

JOHN 1:14 says that:

"The Word became flesh and made his home among us."

Jesus is believed to be God's Word who lived on earth and who, through his death and resurrection, is able to bring God and humanity back into relationship again. God shows how much he loves the world by coming to earth and experiencing terrible suffering and death in order to pay the penalty for human sin. Christians believe that through the death and resurrection of Jesus all humanity can be forgiven and, after death, live eternally with God.

The belief that God came to earth in Jesus, (the Incarnation), to demonstrate his love and to save humanity is a very important and core belief of Christianity. In summary, it shows that God:

- **LOVES THE WORLD** - So much that he would come to earth and live a fully human life to show humanity how to live

- **UNDERSTANDS** - He understands what it is like to live as a human, experiencing the joys and pains of human existence. Philippians 2:6-7 says that though he was God, Jesus took the form of a servant.

- **WAS WILLING** - He was willing to do something about the broken relationship between Him and humanity, which could not be repaired by humanity

- **GAVE HIS ONLY SON** - That God "loved the world so much that He gave his only begotten Son" (John 3:16), so that humanity could be forgiven and redeemed.

A verse in the Bible that sums up Christian belief in the incarnation is from 1 Timothy Chapter 3, verse 16, which says:

"This Christian life is a great mystery, far exceeding our understanding, but some things are clear enough. Jesus appeared in a human body, was proved right by the invisible Spirit, was seen by angels. He was proclaimed by all kinds of peoples, believed in all over the world, taken up into heavenly glory."

For both the Creation and Incarnation sections, read John Chapter 1, verses 1 to 18. In these verses:

- Christ is described as God

- God created the world through Jesus

- God became fully human in Jesus and lived with humanity on earth. We can now see God in Jesus

- Jesus is full of grace and truth

THE PASSION OF CHRIST

The Passion of Christ refers to the last days of Christ on earth, and covers the events of the Last Supper, betrayal, arrest, trial, crucifixion, resurrection and ascension. These events are described in Luke Chapters 22-24, and are specifically remembered by Christians during Holy Week, which is the week before Easter.

The Last Supper took place when Jesus was together with his disciples and friends for a meal. During the meal, Jesus talked about how he soon would be leaving them, and would send them the Holy Spirit. He says that he is going to give his body for them, represented by bread, and that the wine represents the blood he will shed. Shortly after, Jesus suggests that he will be betrayed by someone sitting around the table. This person is **JUDAS**.

The meal becomes very important in Christian tradition as the foundation of the sacrament known as the Eucharist or Holy Communion, where Christians receive the bread and wine to remember the death of Christ and the sacrificing of his body and blood to save humanity from sin. The Eucharist is celebrated in most churches on a regular basis as it represents core beliefs of Christianity and demonstrates Christian understanding of who Jesus is and what he did.

Shortly after the meal, Jesus prays in a garden called **GETHSEMANE**, and is in great pain thinking about the death he is to face. This is important to Christians because it demonstrates how Jesus understands what it feels like to suffer. Following Judas' betrayal, Jesus is then arrested and found guilty of blasphemy by the Jewish religious leaders. The charge of blasphemy against Jesus is because he was believed to be claiming to be the Son of God, which was punishable by death. **PONTIUS PILATE**, the local Roman governor, sentences Jesus to death by crucifixion, which was a form of capital punishment.

Jesus is mocked and beaten and put on a cross, where he dies. The death of Jesus takes place on Friday, and the Christian Church now remembers the day as Good Friday. The use of the word "good" refers to the Christian belief that the death of Jesus was part of God's plan to bring salvation from sin, which is a good thing. Christians understand that through Jesus' suffering and death, people can receive forgiveness for the things they have done wrong against God and others. This also illustrates that Jesus is the rescuer or saviour promised in the Old Testament.

Three days later, in an event now celebrated on Easter Sunday, Christians believe Jesus rose from the dead. The resurrection is central to Christian belief and worship, because it demonstrates that Jesus is part of the Trinity as only God has the power to rise from the dead. It demonstrates that God is all powerful and that death is not the end and that, after death, people can be resurrected to eternal life now that their sins have been forgiven and they have been brought back to God. This belief of being brought back to God is known as atonement.

In Christian belief, 40 days after Jesus was resurrected, he ascended or went up to heaven. After his ascension, the Holy Spirit, whom Jesus had promised, came upon the disciples to enable them to spread the news of Jesus and live as Christians, putting their beliefs into action.

SALVATION AND ATONEMENT

In the Creation story of Genesis Chapter 2 God places a man and a woman in the Garden of Eden, with the explicit instructions not to eat from "the tree of the knowledge of good and evil." God says that if they eat of that tree they shall "surely die." In Genesis 3, Adam and Eve eat from the tree. As a result, the relationship between God and humans, which had been perfect, is broken, and this becomes known as The Fall. Adam and Eve "fall" from their position of closeness to God and are separated from God by sin, that is, their disobedience to God.

In the 4th Century Bishop Augustine, said that this was the story of **ORIGINAL SIN**. The first humans committed the original sin or act of disobedience to God and evil and suffering came into God's perfect world as a result of their actions. Many Christians believe that every human has inherited that sinful nature from the first humans and therefore will disobey God just like Adam and Eve did. This is a law that humans seem to be under - that, despite our best efforts, we will disobey God. Christians believe that the Old Testament commandments and law helped bring order to society, but did not bridge the gap between God and humans.

Because humans are separated from God by sin, something needs to be done to bring them back together again. It is obvious to Augustine that humans cannot do anything about bridging that gap as they have caused it in the first place. It is as if they need to be **BORN AGAIN**, which is a phrase some Christians use. Christians believe that because God is loving and kind, he has acted to restore the relationship between himself and humanity, by coming to earth in the form of Jesus, and making it possible for people to have a fresh start.

Jesus has sacrificed his life to pay the price for humans getting it wrong, and to redeem them. Redeeming something means to make it new again, or to restore it to the way it was. Jesus has made it possible for humans to have a relationship with God again because he has wiped out the consequences of sin. His perfect life and sacrifice has meant God and humans are "at one" again - he has given humanity the chance for **AT-ONE-MENT**. This gift of Jesus is a gift of God's grace to humanity - grace is where we are given something which we don't deserve or cannot get however much we try. Sometimes the death of Jesus is called a ransom, where a price is paid to set another person (humanity) free. It can also be seen as an image from a court of law where an innocent person (Jesus) takes the punishment for someone else who is guilty (humanity).

Because God has sacrificed his life for humanity, it is possible for humans to receive salvation, which is the forgiveness of sins, and eternal life. Humanity is able to be in a relationship with God again, through Christ's death, and then in his presence after death. We no longer have to be separated from God by sin. Jesus died for all humanity, but also rose from death to show that death is not final.

Many Christians say that it is only necessary for a Christian to believe in what Christ has done, and they will receive salvation, and be at one with God in this life and after death. Others believe that it is necessary for people to show that they are sorry for their sins and repent or turn away from them in order to receive Jesus' offer of salvation and be redeemed. Many Christians, particularly Roman Catholics, argue that we have to keep close to God and receive the sacraments, such as baptism and the Eucharist, to be sure of having salvation and eternal life.

The death and resurrection of Jesus, and the atonement, redemption and salvation that comes from them, are significant within Christianity. The act of Jesus rescuing humanity from original sin by sacrificing his life shows the love that God has for his world, as shown in John 3:10-21 and Acts 4:8-12. The belief that Christians can live in relationship with God again is very important, and, again, shows the work of the Trinity, as Christians believe it is the Holy Spirit who helps Christians as to God the Father's grace, and then helps them to follow the teaching and example of Jesus in their lives.

CHRISTIAN ESCHATOLOGY

ESCHATOLOGY is the study of the **END TIMES** or what might happen at the end of the world. Christians believe that there will be a final judgement on all people at the end of time before a new era is brought in where God's kingdom is established.

- Based on teaching in Revelation 21, Christians believe that there will be a kingdom where there will be "no more tears or sadness" and any injustices will be corrected.

- In this new era, God will dwell fully with his people, and the Church will be in union with Jesus, which is described as a marriage.

- Many Christians believe that this era will take place on a renewed earth, where heaven and earth are properly united. This is based on teaching in Revelation 21:1 and Isaiah 65:17.

- There are different understandings of what will take place before the new kingdom is established, with many Christians suggesting that there will be a persecution of anyone who calls themselves Christian. This is based on teaching in Luke 21:12-19.

- As well as persecution, in Luke 21 Jesus says that there will be:

  - wars and uprisings

  - people claiming to be him

  - nation fighting nation

  - earthquakes, famine and disease

  - signs in the sun, moon and the stars

and it is at that time that people will see, "the Son of Man coming in a cloud with power and great glory."

The implications of this teaching is very important for Christians today:

- Because Christians believe that they will, alongside every other person, be judged for how they have lived; this gives importance to how they live now, including how they treat others and the decisions they make and their attitude towards the needy.

- The belief that Jesus will come suddenly also makes Christians aware that they have to be ready at all times, living a life that pleases God.

- This belief gives hope that earthquakes and terrible famines will not have the final word and there is a place with no more pain, sadness or injustice.

Eschatology also concerns what happens after death and what will be revealed at that stage.

Christians believe that there is life after death, although there are different views about what precisely happens when a person dies. Because Jesus was resurrected, if people put their trust in him, then they too will receive new life after death, though not new life back on earth. Reincarnation is not a Christian belief.

Many Christians believe that, after death, although the body stays in the grave, the soul goes immediately to God for judgement. This belief is known as the immortality of the soul. Those who have trusted Jesus and received salvation and cleansing from sins due to the sacrifice of Jesus go to Heaven, where they will be for eternity in the presence of God, with no more pain or sadness. Those who have not trusted Jesus and have not received salvation will go to Hell. Hell is now viewed by many Christians as the absence of God rather than a place of eternal torment and punishment.

Other Christians believe in the resurrection of the body, which will take place at the end of time on Judgement Day when Jesus pronounces God's judgement on every person who has ever lived. At this time, some Christians believe that everyone will go to heaven, which is a theory called universalism, but others believe God will separate people into heaven and hell.

The primary reason for Christian belief in life after death is because of the resurrection of Jesus. Jesus also taught that there are,

- "many rooms in my Father's house which I am going to prepare" (John 14:2)

- He also said to the dying thief on the cross that, after his death, he would be in Paradise with Jesus that same day (Luke 23:43)

- Furthermore, he described himself as the "resurrection and the life", stating that, "he who believes in me will live, even though he dies" (John 11:25-6)

- Throughout history the church has taught that there is life after death and it is stated in both the Nicene and the Apostles Creeds, which are important statements of Christian beliefs

However, some Christians argue that, whilst belief in Christ is important, it is our actions that will be judged, as is shown in the parable of the sheep and the goats (Matthew 25), where the **SHEEP** (the righteous) are given eternal life based on the good deeds they have done rather than what beliefs they have.

- Other Christians do not believe a God of love would allow anyone to go to hell, or that there is such a place

- In contrast, others argue that because God is both loving and just there has to be a place where evil is punished

Roman Catholics believe that after a person dies, if they are in a "state of grace", their soul goes to a place called purgatory. Purgatory is not a place where God decides whether a soul should go to heaven or hell. It is a place where the soul of someone who has died already "in God's grace" is purified before entering heaven, as nothing unclean can enter the presence of God.

However, in 1563, when the beliefs of the Anglican Church (Church of England) were established following the break from the Catholic Church, The Thirty Nine Articles of Religion were developed. These articles forms the basis of Anglican doctrine even today, and in Article 22, the Church of England rejected belief in purgatory, believing it has no basis in the Bible.

Orthodox, Roman Catholic and Protestant teaching argues that there are two judgements. The first one takes place at the time of our individual death, where Jesus judges our soul and we know what our final destiny will be. The second one, the Last Judgement, takes place at the end of the world and is a general judgement of all the nations. This is when Jesus will return to earth to raise the dead, which is called the **PAROUSIA**; in Catholic belief it is at this time that those in purgatory will go to Heaven.

Many Christians believe that, at this time when God raises and judges the dead, they will receive a new resurrected body. St. Paul writes about longing for:

> *"A heavenly body"*

in 2 Corinthians 5:1-10, a Bible passage which ends with the teaching that:

> *"All must appear before the judgement seat of Christ."*

Christians argue that belief in the existence of life after death for all people follows from Christ's own resurrection and his teaching. For Christians:

- **MAKE SENSE** - Belief in life after death helps make sense of this life, particularly when it is not fair, as everything will be fair and just in the end

- **PROVIDES PURPOSE** - In addition, this belief comforts people when they are facing bereavement and loss, and provides a purpose in life, knowing that the actions in this life will be judged and that there is something greater than this life, post death.

See section 4 on life after death for more details on Christian belief in heaven and hell and post-death existence

THE PROBLEM OF EVIL AND SUFFERING

The problem of evil and suffering is a major challenge to Christian belief and raises the question:

"If God is all loving, why is there suffering, pain and evil in the world? Or, to put it another way, what does it say about the nature of God if there is evil and suffering in the world?"

Early Greek philosopher Epicurus put the problem of evil and suffering in the following form:

- Is God willing to prevent suffering, but not able?

- If so, then he is not omnipotent

- Is God able to prevent suffering, but not willing?

- If so, then he is malevolent (evil) and not omnibenevolent

- If God is both able and evil to prevent suffering, then why does it exist?

- If he is neither able nor willing, then why call him God?

This conundrum is sometimes called the **EPICUREAN PARADOX**.

In more recent times, **JL MACKIE** has reformulated the paradox into the form of three statements, known as The Inconsistent Triad. He argues that it is not possible for all three of the following statements to be true at the same time:

- **OMNIBENEVOLENT** - God is all good

- **OMNIPOTENT** - God is all powerful

- **EXISTING** - Evil exists

MACKIE says that if God has the two qualities listed above he would want to remove suffering, and he would have the power to do so. He concludes therefore that as evil does exist, obviously God does not. It is a logical contradiction to suggest that evil and suffering exist and an all good and all powerful God exists.Traditionally, evil and suffering is divided into two types:

- **HUMAN** - Suffering that is caused by humanity, for example, war, murder, torture, etc. is known as moral evil. It is given this name because the person or people who committed the act made a deliberate choice to carry out wrong.

- **NATURAL** - Suffering that is caused by nature, for example, flooding, earthquakes, tsunamis, etc., is called natural evil. It is given this name because the suffering that results is caused by a natural process.

However, natural events such as flooding, can be down to human actions such as deforestation or due to human influenced climate change, so the distinction between the two types of evil is not straightforward. Similarly, illnesses such as cancer might be seen as a natural process in some cases, but caused by heavy smoking in others.

Both forms of evil, which cause immense suffering, are challenging to Christians, and have resulted in some Christians struggling to maintain their faith in the goodness of God. This can affect how Christians feel about God's goodness when they come to worship. Some Christians use Bible passages such as Psalm 103, which suggests God does care for humanity, and is a Father who can be trusted, even if things are not always easy and life is very fragile. The Psalm includes these verses:

"As a father has compassion on his children, so the Lord has compassion on those who fear him; for he knows how we are formed, he remembers that we are dust.

The life of mortals is like grass,
they flourish like a flower of the field;

the wind blows over it and it is gone,
and its place remembers it no more.

But from everlasting to everlasting
the Lord's love is with those who fear him.

The Lord works righteousness
and justice for all the oppressed."

CHRISTIAN RESPONSES TO THE PROBLEM OF EVIL AND SUFFERING

Christian responses to the problem of evil and suffering and the challenges it raises about the nature of God, can be divided into three main areas:

Responses from the Bible

Many of the Psalms in the Old Testament are honest songs about how people seem to suffer, but, in those times of suffering, God has not forgotten or abandoned them. In Psalm 119, the writer says that his:

> *"Soul is weary with sorrow"*

but asks God to:

> *"Strengthen me with your word."*

He goes on to write about how, if a person keeps God's law and resists evil, he will be **DELIVERED** and **PRESERVED**. Even though he says that "the wicked set a trap for me," and asks to be, "redeemed from human oppression," he feels that "the Lord is near" and that "there is peace for those who follow His Law."

The Psalms are very honest, and recognise human pain. In Psalm 119, the author cries out to God, "when will you comfort me?", but, ultimately, clings on to his faith in God. Psalms and other passages like this give Christians great hope that not only does God hear their prayers, but that he will deliver them from their suffering, even if that is not until after death.

One person in the **OLD TESTAMENT** who experienced terrible suffering was a man named **JOB**.

- Although he is a good man with enormous wealth, who is praised by God for his righteousness, God allows Satan to test him. In the Bible, Satan, or the Devil, is present on many occasions, and is seen as a fallen angel who works against God. The testing of Job involves taking his children and many flocks and causing him great pain with body sores and mental torment.

- Although advised to admit that he has done something to deserve his suffering, Job responds by saying that he is innocent. In Job 3, he curses the day he is born, and says that "he has no rest, only turmoil." Throughout the book, where the advice of his friends is of no use, Job clings on to the fact that, somehow, "to God belong wisdom and power."

- At the end of the book, we hear God's voice. He does not defend himself, but suggests that humans have little idea of how omnipotent he is as a Creator of all things and the giver of all life. Job responds by saying that God is way beyond anything he could possibly understand.

Christians learn from this that:

- God allows things to happen which are very difficult for us to understand. Because of this there are no easy solutions to why evil is in the world.

- Suffering seems to be part of life both for people who try to follow God and those who don't

- Job recognises that these things do not change the nature and character of God as righteous, omnipotent and omniscient

The greatest help from the Bible for when Christians experience evil and suffering is the example of Jesus. As Christians believe that Jesus was God in human form, they believe that God knows what it is like to feel pain, sorrow and anguish. There are times in the New Testament when Jesus is recorded as:

- Deeply distressed when a friend dies (John 11:33)

- In great agony when he knows his own death is near (Luke 22:44)

The belief that God experienced great pain gives comfort to Christian during difficult times, and helps them in worship, as it reminds Christians that God knows about human experience, with all its joys and pains. The death and resurrection of Jesus gives Christians hope that suffering and death is not the end, but that there is a better after life in Heaven, where there will be no more tears, pain or suffering.

Responses in Christian belief

One major Christian response to the problem of evil and suffering is to believe that humans have free will, which was first given to Adam and Eve. Humans are not forced to make good choices, which means that some choices we make are not wise and result in suffering. However, to have free will is a good thing, and can result in good choices, such as freely choosing to love someone. Christians believe that God shows his goodness in giving humanity freedom to choose, as it allows us to live fully, make mistakes and learn from them, and not live like robots.

Another Christian response is to believe that this life on earth is a time for our souls to develop. Irenaeus, an early Christian teacher, believed that this life was a way of shaping our souls so that every experience of life, even the painful ones, helps us to develop and grow closer to God. This theory sometimes calls life a vale of soul-making. Although we pass through a vale (valley) and at times it is dark, if we learn the lessons in those times, then the journey shapes our souls to develop characteristics such as patience, compassion and empathy.

Practical Christian responses to suffering and evil

- Christians believe that one of the most important ways to respond to evil and suffering is to show the love of God by caring for others.
- Christian charities, such as World Vision, The Salvation Army and CAFOD (Catholic Agency for Overseas Development) help millions of people who are experiencing the consequences of natural disaster, poverty, war and other events that have resulted in suffering
- On a local level, many Christians choose to work in caring professions, such as nursing or social care, or help out in their communities by visiting the elderly or working with the homeless
- Many Christians regularly support relief efforts by raising or giving money.
- A second practical response is for Christians to pray for others and the world. Many Christians pray that God will comfort those who are in pain and suffering, and that peace will come to areas which are in conflict. Other Christians, particularly those from the Charismatic churches, will pray directly for people, that God will heal them.
- Are Christian responses to suffering and evil successful or convincing?

Responses from the Bible

- Many Christians find comfort and hope from the Bible, and sections such as the Psalms and Job, and the belief that God knows about their suffering and pain. They are supported by the idea that, as seen in the life of Jesus, God knows what pain is like
- However, this does not stop the fact that there is suffering and pain, so why doesn't God stop it? Christians might wonder if God can actually stop it
- It might also make Christians wonder why God made a world in which enormous evil and suffering takes place.

Responses in Christian belief

- Because of free will, Christians believe that humanity is responsible for much of the suffering that goes on in the world

- Free will is a good thing, even though the consequences of that free will might result in evil and suffering, and things such as murder and war. Free will also results in kindness and compassion

- However, God is omniscient so must have known that humanity would abuse the gift of free will, so is it God's fault that suffering takes place?

- It could be argued that learning our lessons from suffering so that our soul develops is a very painful way of growth and development - perhaps too painful for many people.

Practical Christian responses to suffering and evil

- Christians do not believe that prayer and charity will stop suffering. These are practical ways in which they can show the love of God and compassion for others

- However, many atheists might suggest that it is strange to pray to God to stop suffering when he is the one who allowed it in the first place

- Christians might respond by arguing that at a time of suffering and loss, people do not want a set of explanations about why they are suffering, and why God does or does not seem to answer prayer, but to know someone is there caring for them and helping them get things back together again, if possible.

NEED MORE HELP ON BELIEFS?

Use your phone to scan this QR code

Marriage & the Family

KEYWORDS

- **ANNULMENT** - A declaration by the Church that a marriage can be ended because it was not lawful or true

- **ATHEIST** - A person who does not believe that God or Gods exist

- **BLENDED FAMILY** - A family unit made up of a married couple and their children, including a child or children from a previous marriage/s

- **CIVIL PARTNERSHIP** - A legal relationship between two people of the same sex that gives them the same rights as a married couple

- **COHABITATION** - Living together without being married

- **CONTRACEPTION** - The deliberate use of artificial methods or other techniques to prevent pregnancy from occurring

- **DIVORCE** - The formal ending of a marriage by a legal process

- **EXTENDED FAMILY** - A nuclear family and their close relatives, such as the children's grandparents, aunts and uncles living together

- **FAMILY PLANNING** - Planning how many children to have in a relationship and when

- **HOMOSEXUALITY** - Sexual attraction to a person of the same sex

- **HUMANAE VITAE** - 1968 document from the Pope guiding Roman Catholics about family life and procreation

- **HUMANISM** - A system of values that emphasises the value of human beings, and which prefers critical reasoning to religion

- **MARRIAGE** - A legally accepted union between two people as partners in a relationship

- **NUCLEAR FAMILY** - A couple and their children, living together as a unit

- **PARISH** - An area cared for by a priest and the local church

- **PRE-MARITAL SEX** - Sex before marriage

- **PROCREATION** - Making a new life

- **REMARRIAGE** - Marrying again after a previous marriage ends

- **RITE OF PASSAGE** - A ceremony or event to mark an important stage in someone's life, eg the transition from childhood to adulthood

- **SAME SEX MARRIAGE** - Legally accepted union between two people of the same sex as partners in a relationship

- **SINGLE PARENT FAMILY** - A lone parent and dependent child/children living as a family unit

- **SITUATION ETHICS** - A method of trying to do the most loving thing in each situation

MARRIAGE

Within Christianity, marriage is regarded as very significant. Emphasis is placed on the role that committed and faithful marriages make to stable family life and society.

Marriage is supported in the Bible and Christian teaching:

- **UNITED INTO ONE** - In Genesis 2:24, at the beginning of creation, the man and woman are joined to each other, and "united into one." Many Christians think that this signifies the importance that God places on marriage, as this verse comes at the very beginning of the Bible and God's plan for humanity.

- **GENESIS** - In his own teaching about marriage in Mark 10:6-9 Jesus repeats the verse from Genesis to stress the importance and central role of marriage.

- **HOLY** - Marriage is regarded by many Christians as a sacrament, which is an occasion or event where God gives his grace. This highlights the sanctity of marriage, where the relationship is regarded as holy, meaning that it is something to be kept pure and honouring to God. In Hebrews 13:4, the author writes,

   "Let marriage be held in honour among all, and let the marriage bed be undefiled, for God will judge the sexually immoral and adulterous."

- **SEXUAL RELATIONSHIPS** - For many Christians, marriage is the only appropriate setting for sexual relationships, as the sexual intimacy takes place within a committed partnership already blessed by God. Christians believe God is love and wants people to give and receive love, which is what happens in marriage.

- **PURPOSE** - Protestant Christianity has emphasised that the role and purpose of marriage is to bring comfort and joy to each of the partners, and stability in society. In Protestant and Catholic Churches it is also the relationship God has designed for the purpose of procreation and family life. For all Christians, marriage is intended to last until the death of one of the spouses.

- **HETEROSEXUAL** - Traditional Christian teaching regards marriage to be between one man and one woman.

However, **ATHEIST** and **HUMANIST** attitudes challenge the need to place such emphasis on marriage. In the past 50 years society has changed, meaning that in the 21st Century people should be free to enter relationships which involve different types of family life:

- **CHOICE** - People should be free to choose whether to have children without necessarily being in a long-term relationship to the father or mother of the child.

- **ANY RELATIONSHIP** - People should be free to raise children in a variety of settings. This could be within a cohabiting partnership, same sex relationship or as a single parent who has chosen to raise children without a partner. Marriage is no longer as important for fulfilling this purpose.

- **NO PRESSURE** - There should be no pressure for people to make a commitment to marriage, and some atheists and humanists argue that the promise "until death us do part" is unrealistic. All that matters is that humans treat each other with respect in their relationships and look out for each other's good.

In response, whilst believing marriage is still vitally important, some Christians, in denominations such as the Methodist Church, teach that a long-term, stable and committed relationship can be an appropriate setting for sexual relationships and family life. The Church of England no longer calls living together before marriage as **LIVING IN SIN**, whilst the Roman Catholic Church will marry people who have been living together and have children before marriage, as long as one of the partners is a Roman Catholic. The United Reformed Church now allows its priests to conduct same sex marriages.

Christian teaching still emphasises that marriage is the primary setting for stable family life, which God intends for the welfare of children and society.

SEXUAL RELATIONSHIPS

Marriage and sex

Christians teach that sex should be loving and a sign of **COMMITMENT**, and should take place within marriage, to bring unity and joy to the couple and for procreation:

- **NOT DIRTY** - God instructed Adam and Eve to be "fruitful and multiply", so sex is not seen as dirty or unclean.

- **EXPRESSION OF LOVE** - Christians teach God's plan for sex is that it is an expression of love within marriage between two faithful partners.

- **NO SEX WITHOUT MARRIAGE** - As well as being an expression of a loving marriage, the potential outcome of sex is so significant that pre-marital sex or adultery is not God's plan for sex.

- **NO PROMISCUITY** - All Christians disapprove of promiscuity.

- **CONSIDER MARRIAGE** - Some Christians argue that a long-term, stable and committed relationship can be a fitting setting for sexual relationships, but would encourage the partners to consider marriage. Others, however, believe that all sex outside marriage, even if the partners intend to get married, is wrong.

Christian attitudes towards homosexuality

Some Christians believe that homosexuality is wrong because:

- **AGAINST GOD'S PLAN** - It goes against God's plan for sexual relationships and marriage, which should be between one woman and one man

- **NO BABIES** - Homosexual relationships cannot naturally procreate, which Christians believe is a core purpose of marriage

- **CONDEMNED** - It is condemned in the Bible, which states that men who did not honour God, "abandoned the natural function for that which is unnatural" and, "men with men committed indecent acts" for which they "received due penalty" (Romans 1:21, 26-27)

Some Christians believe that the teaching of 1 Corinthians 6:9 applies today. In that verse, homosexuality is included in a list of actions that exclude people from the Kingdom of God. In verses 18 and 19 of the same chapter, Christians are encouraged to **FLEE IMMORALITY** (wrong actions) as their "body is a temple of the Holy Spirit."

Some Christians believe that these verses are still a source of authority for today, and that they disallow any sexual relationships outside heterosexual marriage.

However, other Christians argue that:

- **NATURAL** - Homosexuality is natural and people should be allowed to express their sexuality

- **LOVE** - God is a God of love, so celebrates love wherever it is shown

- **EQUALITY** - Everyone is born in the image of God, and equal, so should be shown respect

- **NO DISCRIMINATION** - Jesus said that we should love one another without discrimination

- **TEACHING** - Teaching on homosexuality should be changed to reflect changing attitudes in the UK

Atheist and Humanist views

Atheists and humanists argue that people should be free to express their sexuality in different ways, as long as that is in ways that does not hurt the other person or persons involved.

- **RESPECT** - A person's sexuality should be respected

- **EQUALITY** - People should be allowed equal access to legal rights, such as marriage

- **OUTDATED** - The Church's teaching is outdated and based on belief in a supernatural deity and religious dogma, not reasoned argument

- **FAIRNESS** - In the 21st Century, discrimination on the grounds of sexuality has no place

Mixed views and responses in different churches

- **CHURCH OF ENGLAND** - Same sex marriage is not allowed, and same sex relationships are not blessed. Permission is given for priests and Bishops to enter into a civil partnership as long as the relationship is celibate.

- **METHODIST CHURCH** - Considering whether to allow same sex marriage, whilst the United Reformed Church has decided to let its local churches decide if they want to conduct same sex marriages.

- **ROMAN CATHOLIC CHURCH** - Does not allow for same sex marriages or bless same sex unions. Homosexual desires are not sinful, but are if they are acted out. It argues that homosexual people should be given respect and care, but that homosexual behaviour is against God's law, which does not change.

- **QUAKERS** - Argue that to reject people because of their sexual behaviour is a denial of God's creation, and accept homosexual relationships

CHRISTIAN TEACHING ON MARRIAGE AND FAMILY LIFE

All Christians believe that the family is very significant because **IT IS**:

- **BUILDING BLOCK** - The basic building block that God has designed for the welfare of society

- **PROCREATION** - The best place for procreation, and a safe environment for the growth and development of children

- **RIGHT/WRONG** - The place where children receive teaching about right and wrong

- **DEMONSTRATION** - Where children see Christian values, beliefs and practices demonstrated

- **VIRTUES** - The place where virtues such as patience, kindness and compassion can be developed

- **VULNERABILITY** - The place where the safety and welfare of vulnerable, young and old members of the family can be lovingly assured

The reason Christians believe the family is important is because the Bible and the teaching of the Church stress the significant role it plays.

The Bible

In Ephesians 6:1-4, the relationship between children and parents is outlined as one which should be mutually respectful. Children are taught to **HONOUR THEIR MOTHER AND FATHER**.

Fathers are instructed not to:

"Provoke their children to anger by the way they treat them."

Rather, fathers are told to:

"Bring children up with discipline and instruction that comes from the Lord."

The verses go on to say that the honouring of parents results in a long life, and that things will go well for those who follow God's teaching in the family home.

The Church of England

The CoE stresses that marriage is for the joy and comfort of the partners in it, and for the joy of children. It teaches that:

"Children thrive, grow and develop within the love and safeguarding of a family. Within the family we care for the young, the old and those with needs. Families offer commitment, fun, love companionship and security."

The Roman Catholic Church teaches that the family is blessed by God as the union which results in new life through procreation. In the Catechism (Catholic Church teaching) it notes that:

"The family is the community in which, from childhood, one can learn moral values, begin to honour God and make good use of freedom."

Many Christians regard the **TRADITIONAL NUCLEAR FAMILY** as God's design for family life. However, attitudes towards family life have changed within society and are changing within the Church.

SUPPORT FOR THE FAMILY IN THE LOCAL PARISH

Recognising that there are many models of family life in the 21st Century, such as single parent, cohabiting parents with children, same-sex marriages, extended and blended, the Church, through its work in local parishes, attempts to support families and parents by:

- **WELCOME** - Offering welcome and support to all parents through weekly parent and toddler groups

- **GUIDANCE** - Offering parenting and marriage guidance classes

- **EDUCATION** - Providing Christian education on marriage and family life through schools, where the local priest will often visit and be on the board of governors

- **FAMILY SERVICES** - Holding family services in the local church on special occasions such as at Easter and Christmas

- **CEREMONIES** - Offering to conduct ceremonies which mark rites of passage. These rites of passage, such as baptism, confirmation and marriage are outlined by the local priest when he meets the family and explains Christian beliefs and teachings and the significance of the step being taken.

All churches stress that the parish consists of everyone in a geographical area, and not just those who attend church. This is based on Jesus' teaching that Christians should love their neighbours and that everyone is their neighbour.

Christians attempt to do this whilst still trying to uphold Christian teaching on the sanctity of marriage, sexual relationships and family life, and therefore might encourage cohabiting parents to consider marriage.

The Church recognises that one of the most vulnerable groups in society is children.

In Matthew 19:13-14 Jesus teaches that children should not be discouraged or forbidden from meeting him, even though the followers of Jesus at the time thought he would be too busy for them. Because of this, the Christian church organises:

- **SUNDAY SCHOOL** - Classes especially for children

- **FAMILY WORSHIP SERVICES** - That include children

- **SPECIAL EVENTS** - For children and young people such as: Soul Survivor, and Warrior

Camps, where emphasis is placed on relevant worship and teaching about central aspects of Christian belief and practice.

National Christian organisations that attempt to support and encourage the welfare of marriage and family life include:

- **CATHOLIC CARE** - Provides a team of social workers specialising in family care, who deliver practical support to children, young people and their families, regardless of the particular family structure those young people are in.

- **CARE FOR THE FAMILY** - Which is committed to:

  "Strengthening family life and helping those who are hurting because of family difficulties ... bringing hope and compassion."

- **THE CATHOLIC MARRIAGE ADVISORY SERVICE**

- **THE METHODIST HOMES FOR THE AGED**

- **THE CHILDREN'S SOCIETY**

Whilst the traditional Christian family model is not to live in extended families, Christians are taught to care for their parents as they become more vulnerable, and may use the services above or care for them locally with the support of the parish.

FAMILY PLANNING AND BIRTH CONTROL

There are different attitudes within Christianity towards using artificial methods of contraception:

Sacred Union

The Roman Catholic belief is that sex expresses a sacred union between a man and a woman. Through this act of love, God brings about new life, and nothing should interfere with God's creative act. Therefore, every time a married couple have sexual intercourse, there should be the possibility of new life being created and no artificial contraception should be used. Procreation is a core purpose of marriage.

Pro-Life

Catholic teaching is pro-life, and is informed by documents such as Humanae Vitae, which outlined teaching on marriage, responsible parenting and the regulation of birth. The teaching stressed that man is:

> *"Not free to act as they choose in the service of transmitting life … but bound to ensure that what they do corresponds to the will of God the Creator."*

> *"Every marital act [of sex] must retain its intrinsic relationship to the procreation of human life."*

> *"The direct interruption [ie artificial contraception] of the generative process … is to be absolutely excluded as a lawful means of regulating the number of children."*

Humanae Vitae

This means that man cannot **PLAY GOD** or go against God's natural law in deciding when a child is conceived, but must allow for that possibility every time sex takes place.

The teaching of **HUMANAE VITAE** allows for a husband and wife to "space out" when they have their children by having intercourse during those times when a woman is less likely to conceive. This is a natural method of contraception.

Humanae Vitae warned that use of artificial birth control would result in an increase in casual sex, without mutual love and respect for procreation, and this would undermine family life.

Some Evangelical Christians support the above view, believing that it is God and not man who decides if sexual intercourse results in pregnancy.

Many Protestant groups believe that the act of sex is also to bring unity and joy in marriage and does not always have to be for the purpose of procreation. They allow artificial contraception to be used which prevents a pregnancy from commencing, such as condoms or the pill. In addition to enabling them to plan a family, in times of illness, financial difficulty or stress, or if a pregnancy might be harmful to the mother or family, a couple should still have the possibility of sexual joy and therefore could use contraception.

Most Christians believe that once a pregnancy has begun it should be carried through to full term, and therefore, whilst they might support artificial contraception that prevents sperm meeting egg, they would disagree with contraceptives such as the morning after pill, or using abortion as a form of contraception.

Situation Ethics

Some Christians believe Christ taught that doing the most loving thing in every situation is what is important. This is known as Situation Ethics:

- **AGAPE LOVE** - The love to be shown to others is known as agape love and tries to promote the best outcome for another person. This love avoids people doing what they think is the most loving thing just for them, and is an unselfish love.

- **CONTRACEPTION IS LOVING** - If the most loving thing for a couple is to express their love for each other in sex, but they are not ready for a child or they already have many children, or it could be dangerous for the woman to get pregnant, then the most loving, (agape) thing to do could be to use artificial contraception.

- **SHOULD GOD DECIDE?** - Roman Catholic teaching has criticised Situation Ethics as allowing human beings to become God in deciding what is loving and what is not.

- **SEX & PROCREATION** - Catholics argue that God has already laid down a moral law that will result in the most benefit for human beings, and should be followed. Sex should not be separated from procreation.

- **UNFORSEEN CONSEQUENCES** - Actions, even if loving, should not be decided in each situation, as this could result in unforeseen and unwanted consequences.

- **GOD OF LOVE** - Jesus did not say that Christians should decide in each situation to do the most loving thing, but follow a God of love. Jesus, and teaching in the Bible, upholds the sanctity of marriage as the place of sexual intercourse and family life.

Atheist and Humanist Responses

Most atheists and humanists do not object to artificial contraception, stressing the need for the child to be wanted and loved. This is because:

- **NO NATURAL LAW** - God has not laid down any laws for procreation and contraception

- **RESPONSIBLE ADULTS** - The decision to have children is therefore up to the people who have sexual intercourse

- **REASONED CONTROL** - The important thing is not following any religious law but allowing people to exercise reasoned control over their decisions

Atheist and humanist responses stress the right of the couple to choose when and if to have children and when to start a family in a responsible approach to sex and family life. In the 19th Century, humanist **JOHN STUART MILL** promoted birth control as a responsible approach towards sex. The approach would support human freedom and not the need to follow a Deity or Divine Law.

Humanists and atheists **DISAGREE** with the Roman Catholic Church as they allow artificial contraception to be used when one or more of the couple carry genetic disorders or conditions that could be passed on through sex. They would also agree with the use of birth control by artificial contraception if a person wants to have sex but is too young or not ready to have a child.

DIVORCE AND REMARRIAGE

In data from the Office for National Statistics, (2013), 42% of marriages **END IN DIVORCE**, which is the lowest rate of divorce for 40 years.

There are different attitudes within Christianity towards divorce and remarriage:

- **SACREMENT** - Many Protestant Christians recognise marriage as a sacrament, where God's grace is given. Solemn promises are made to each other and the couple have every intention of keeping those promises.

- **BROKEN PROMISES** - However, sometimes promises are broken through things such as adultery or unreasonable behaviour. In such cases, many churches offer counselling and attempt to help the couple reconcile their differences. If this cannot happen, and the marriage is irretrievably broken, then the Church of England and other Protestant Churches allow a couple to divorce. Sometimes, allowing a harmful marriage to end can be the lesser of two evils.

- **REMARRIAGE** - If, after careful marriage preparation, the partners from a divorce wish to marry again (either each other, or another partner), then, in exceptional circumstances and on a case by case basis, decided by the local priest, remarriage in a Protestant Church is permitted. Prince Charles and Camilla Parker Bowles were not permitted to marry in church as adultery had led to the breakup of Charles' first marriage to Princess Diana.

- **UNFAITHFULNESS** - Protestant Churches believe that Jesus allowed for divorce in the case of one partner being unfaithful. In Matthew 9 Jesus says that God allows divorce in this circumstance because people are "hard hearted" and don't live up to God's original intention for marriage. God is loving and forgiving if people do genuinely regret their actions.

Roman Catholic attitudes towards divorce and remarriage are different

Following careful preparation by the priest, marriage in the Catholic Church is entered into as the lifelong union of the partners and God in a sacrament where God is present by his grace.

Marriage is therefore both a legal and spiritual bond. Because God is joined to the couple in a spiritual bond, a legal ceremony cannot break it, and therefore divorce is not allowed. In technical language:

> *"The Church does not recognise a civil divorce because the State cannot dissolve what is indissoluble."*

The Catholic Church accepts Jesus' teaching in Matthew 19:6, which states that:

> *"What God has joined together, let no one separate."*

In addition, St. Paul says in 1 Corinthians 7:10 that:

> *"The wife should not separate from her husband … and the husband should not divorce his wife."*

Divorce attempts to break promises made with God and separate **ONE FLESH**, which is not possible. What is permitted, after serious questioning and a long time, is for a marriage to be annulled. This is where a marriage is ended because it was never true or lawful in the first place:

- **MENTAL INCAPACITY** - One partner was mentally unable to understand their vows

- **FORCED MARRIAGE** - One partner was forced into the marriage

- **NO CHILDREN** - One partner didn't intend to have children

- **NO CONSUMMATION** - The marriage has not been consummated

- **ANNULMENT** - An annulment is not a divorce. Following the annulment of the marriage by the Catholic Church, the couple must also get a civil (legal) divorce

- **DIVORCE NOT RECOGNISED** - Divorced people who have not had their marriage annulled cannot be remarried in a Catholic Church. Because divorce is not recognised, the Church regards the person as married and adultery would take place if they married again.

- **WIDOWHOOD** - If a person's original marriage has not been annulled, the person can only be remarried if their original spouse has died

Non-religious approaches to marriage and divorce

Some people do not want to make promises before God in a Church on their wedding day, as that would go against their beliefs.

▸ Humanist Weddings

HUMANIST weddings ceremonies can include readings, music, a symbolic ritual and the sharing of vows chosen by the couple, but have no reference or promises made to a God. Humanist weddings are not legally binding in England, and therefore the couple have to carry out legal requirements at a registry office. Though both humanists and atheists accept the seriousness of the commitments made in marriage, it is not regarded as sacred and therefore divorce is permitted. This is better than an unhappy and painful relationship.

▸ **Situation Ethics**

The approach to marriage and divorce within Situation Ethics is based around the law of love. Nothing, like marriage or divorce, is labelled "good" or "bad" by itself. A marriage or divorce is only good if it demonstrates **AGAPE LOVE**.

The mature person asks what is the most loving action in each situation.

Situation Ethicists suggest that Jesus' teaching allows for divorce as he wants the most loving thing in each situation.

Love is the only thing that is always good, not rules or traditions, and therefore divorce is allowed where it is the most loving thing.

Christian Responses to Humanists

Christians respond to atheist and humanist approaches to marriage by suggesting that God is the source of all love, so to not make any reference to God in a marriage service misses out the foundation of all love and happiness, and does not offer the support that God and the Church can bring to a relationship.

Many Christians would agree that love is the most important thing in every situation. However, many would feel uncomfortable with what really motivates the ending of a marriage, and whether it really is the most loving thing to do, or if there are other less admirable motives. Many Christians regard Situation Ethics as disrespectful to the unchanging laws laid out in the Bible and have concerns about the power it gives to humans to decide whether or not to follow those laws.

THE EQUALITY OF MEN AND WOMEN IN THE FAMILY

Christians regard men and women as equal due to the teaching in Genesis when God created the first man and woman. GENESIS 1:27, says that God:

> *"Created humankind in his image; in the image of God he created them; male and female he created them."*

As this is part of the first chapter of the Bible, many Christians think that this means that God's plan is for men and women to be equal as they are both made in his image.

For some Christians this means that all roles should be open equally to men and women, including roles within the family. Christians who take this stance suggest that Bible teaching such as Ephesians 5:22-24 should be read very carefully. The verses say:

> *"Wives, be subject to your husbands as you are to the Lord. For the husband is head of the wife just as Christ is head of the church. Just as the church is subject to Christ, so also wives ought to be, in everything, to their husbands."*

Some Christians argue that if these verses are taken without the next verse. the teaching would place women under the authority of their husbands. In verse 25, the passage goes on to say:

> *"Husbands, love your wives, just as Christ loved the church and gave himself up for her."*

With this verse added, many Christians argue that it actually teaches that marriage is about mutual service, as a husband is willing to give his life for his wife and serve her in the same way Christ sacrificially served the church.

Christians who take this stance argue that this allows Church teaching to be in line with what takes place in 21st Century society where men and women can have equal roles in the family, are both able to go out to work and have careers, and have equal responsibility for the care of their children.

Other Christians, particularly within some Evangelical and Baptist Churches, regard the primary responsibility of woman as caring for the home and family.

Some Christians support this view with different verses from the Creation story, where, after the Fall, God says to Eve that:

> *"Your desire shall be for your husband, and he shall rule over you."*

1 Timothy 2:13-14 says that,

> *"Adam was formed first, then Eve; and Adam was not deceived, but the woman was deceived and became a transgressor"* (sinner)

These teachings are used to suggest an order in the family where the man is the head of the house and wage earner, and women have the role of serving the house and family. For many years, this was the traditional role of men and women in a Christian family. Whilst men and women in this view are regarded as equal before God, they are given different roles according to God's plan for family life.

In response, many Christians recognise that throughout history the teaching that Eve was the one who was weak and gave in to sin has caused much distress and accusations that Church teaching discriminates against women. For many Christians today, the Fall is a symbolic story of how all people fall short of God's standard, but can still share in God's love.

EQUALITY means that men and women have both equal opportunities and responsibilities in family life. Many Christians value the freedom of choice, arguing that if a partner chooses to be at home to care for the family, this is just as worthy as a career.

Describing family life, Pope John Paul II wrote that:

> *"All members of the family, each according to his or her own gift, have the grace and responsibility of building day by day the community of persons making a family a school of deeper humanity."*

St Paul, in 1 Corinthians 7:3, taught that both partners have equal responsibilities so that:

> *"The husband should please his wife as a husband. The wife should please her husband as a wife"*

Many Christians regard these teachings from the Bible and leaders of the Church as supporting total equality in the roles between men and women in the family setting.

CHRISTIAN TEACHING ABOUT GENDER PREJUDICE AND DISCRIMINATION

Christians are against gender prejudice and discrimination. **GALATIANS 3:23-29** teaches that:

> *"You are now children of God because you trust in Christ. God does not see you as a Jew or as a Greek. He does not see you as a servant or a person free to work. He does not see you as a man or as a woman. You are all one in Christ."*

Christians try to follow this teaching and the example of Jesus, who treated women with great respect, going against many conventions of his culture and the way his own society regarded women. He gave dignity to women when they were not normally considered an important part of society.

Examples from history of Christian opposition to gender prejudice and discrimination:

- **WOLLSTONECRAFT** - In 1792, Mary Wollstonecraft published **A VINDICATION OF THE RIGHTS OF WOMEN**, arguing for the equal education of women. This was a radical thing to do at the time. Although she rejected much traditional teaching of the Church, she was motivated to write for better rights for women because of her belief that God had created men and women equal.

- **SUFFRAGETTES** - Although the Church of England did not officially support the movement to get women the vote, the **CHURCH LEAGUE FOR WOMEN'S SUFFRAGE** and the **CATHOLIC WOMEN'S SUFFRAGE LEAGUE** had over 5,000 members in 1914. Many suffragettes used reasons from the Bible to support their cause.

- **GLOBAL INEQUALITY** - Across the world Christian Aid is working to challenge gender norms and power structures, which it argues are a major factor in the continuing inequality between men and women. This inequality fails girls and women and stops them from reaching their potential.

- **ROLE OF WOMEN** - Christians support equality but disagree about the role of women in the Church

- **WOMEN PRIESTS** - Many Protestant Churches, such as The Church of England, Methodist and The Salvation Army ordain women as priests. From 1986 to 1993, the leader of The Salvation Army was a female Officer (priest). In 2015, The Church of England appointed its **FIRST FEMALE BISHOP**. However, the Roman Catholic Church does not ordain women. There are several areas of disagreement between churches on the question of the ordination of women.

NEED MORE HELP ON MARRIAGE & THE FAMILY?

Use your phone to scan this QR code

Living the Christian Life

KEYWORDS

- **ADVENT** - The season including the four Sundays before Christmas marking preparation for the coming of Christ

- **APOSTLES CREED** - An important statement of early Christian belief, originating in AD390 and still used in Christian churches today

- **AUTHORITY** - Having power to give guidance, commands and direction

- **BAPTISM** - Christian service or rite, where water is either sprinkled on the head, or a person is fully immersed in water, to symbolise purification and admission into the Christian Church. A sacrament

- **BOOK OF COMMON PRAYER** - The title given to a number of prayer books used in the Church of England to instruct worship

- **CONVERSION** - A change in which a person adopts a new religion or faith

- **DOCTRINE** - A set of beliefs held and taught by the Church

- **ECUMENISM** - A movement trying to promote greater unity between Christians and Christian churches

- **EUCHARIST** - Christian service where bread and wine are consecrated (set apart for sacred use) and consumed. Literally meaning "thanksgiving". A sacrament also known as the Lord's Supper or Holy Communion

- **EVANGELICAL** - A type of Christianity which emphasises the authority of the Bible and the need for personal conversion to Christ

- **GOSPEL** - The teaching of Christ, written in the Bible by Matthew, Mark, Luke and John

- **LENT** - A 40-day period of fasting and prayer observed by many Christians in preparation for Easter

- **LITURGY** - A form of worship using a set script and order

- **MASS** - The act of worship in which the Eucharist is celebrated in the Roman Catholic Church, (and some Protestant churches)

- **NICENE CREED** - An important statement of Christian belief originating in AD325 and still stated in Christian churches today

- **PILGRIMAGE** - A meaningful journey made to a holy place

- **PRAYER** - An attempt to contact God, usually involving words

- **RECONCILIATION** - Restoring friendly relations between people or groups who have been against each other

- **SACRAMENT** - An event or ceremony where God's grace is received

- **THE THIRTY NINE ARTICLES** - Historical statements that outline the accepted doctrine of the Church of England

- **WORSHIP** - Adoration, love and honour to God - in Christian churches through liturgy or free expression, prayer, music or other forms

THE PRACTICE AND SIGNIFICANCE OF CHRISTIAN WORSHIP

There are a wide variety of ways in which Christians worship, and different churches have different traditions. These are based on sources of authority, primarily the tradition of the Church, which is an important source of authority particularly for Roman Catholics, and the Bible, which, for many within the Protestant tradition, is the primary source of authority.

Liturgical Worship

Many churches, particularly when celebrating the sacraments such as the Eucharist and baptism use a set order of service and a pattern of words for worship, which is known as the liturgy.

This liturgy can take the form of:

- **SET PRAYERS** - The Priest leading the congregation in set prayer/s

- **QUOTATIONS** - Reference to or quotation from a passage from the Bible or a Creed

- **RITE OF PASSAGE** - Introduction to the sacrament or rite of passage being taken

- **CONSECRATION** - Preparation and consecration of the elements (eg bread and wine) involved in the sacrament

- **SPEAKING OUT LOUD** - Particular words being said during the actual sacrament. For example, words similar to those said by Jesus at the Last Supper

- **INVITATIONS TO RESPOND** - Invitations for the congregation to respond with certain actions or words at designated places in the liturgy. For example, the congregation being told when to go forward to the altar to receive the bread and wine and how to receive it, which can be different according to different church traditions.

Actions which accompany the celebration of the sacrament or other acts of liturgical worship include bowing in the direction of the altar, the use of incense, and the making of the sign of the cross, all of which signify the respect for and importance of what is taking place in worship.

As Baptism and the Eucharist celebrate the central beliefs about Jesus' life and death, and the way in which a person is welcomed into the Church, these sacraments are given great honour through the specific words and traditions of the liturgy.

During important Church Festivals or Celebrations, such as Holy Week or Advent, many churches have particular rituals on certain days. One example of this, which takes place in both Anglican and Roman Catholic churches, is called The Stations of the Cross. A person travels to 14 "stations" in the church, which follow a particular order. Each station is marked with a prayer, which is said in front of an icon.

Each stage and icon commemorates a different event in Jesus' last day on earth and this mini pilgrimage normally takes place during Lent on Wednesdays and Fridays, and especially on Good Friday, the day of the year upon which the events occurred.

Anglican (Church of England) Churches make use of the Book of Common Prayer. This is the:

> *"Traditional service book of the Church of England, and is central to its faith."*

It was:

> *"Compiled in the 16th century by* **THOMAS CRANMER** *… and remains at the heart of Anglican worship. It is the official doctrinal standard of the Church of England."*

This important work, moderated in 1662, guides priests and worship leaders on the liturgy to use for:

- **SUNDAY WORSHIP**

- **SPECIAL CELEBRATIONS** - Such as Easter and Advent

- **SPECIAL EVENTS** - Such as baptisms, marriages and funerals

and is closely based on the Bible.

Phrases in the CBP such as "til death us do part" and "peace in our time" have become part of the English language.

In Roman Catholic Churches, pictures and statues of saints are often seen, and used to help Catholics pray. Roman Catholics can ask saints to pray for them.

Reasons for using liturgical worship

- **WISDOM & AUTHORITY** - The words used link back to the teachings and events of the Bible, which is an important source of wisdom and authority in Christianity. Actions such as the Stations of the Cross reflect practices that have been carried out for 2,000 years in Christian worship.

- **TRADITIONAL** - It ensures that the Church stays true to its doctrines, which have been used in Christian tradition and outlined in historic creeds.

- **GIVES STRUCTURE** - It gives a structure and order to worship, which becomes very familiar and comforting. In 1987, Terry Waite, who worked for the Church of England, was taken hostage. He was kept in solitary confinement for four years and during that time what he remembered was the pattern of the liturgy which he had heard regularly in church, and this comforted and supported him.

- **SENSE OF BELONGING** - Some Christians use liturgical worship when worshipping and praying on their own, following the readings and prayers that are set down in the Church liturgical calendar. This gives Christians a sense of belonging to the worldwide Church and reminds them of the beliefs and traditions that have survived for centuries.

Non-liturgical worship

In recent years the Church of England has allowed for more informal acts of worship to be conducted in local parishes, as long as they do not contradict Church doctrine. Suggestions for services are laid out in a book of guidance, New Patterns for Worship, where headings and suggested texts are provided, with interpretation allowed for by the local priest.

An informal Service of the Word, where the priest will choose readings and plan worship carefully around a theme can be used to prepare people for the more formal celebration of the Eucharist. This kind of service is a link between liturgical and non-liturgical worship.

Many other churches have a set pattern of what will take place in a worship service, but the leader will decide what goes into each of the stages. For example, times of prayer in a Salvation Army service are often not scripted and anyone can pray during such times. Many Protestants find great comfort from familiar hymns used during worship.

In Charismatic and Pentecostal Churches liturgy is rarely used. This is because the emphasis is on the congregation being free to be led by the Holy Spirit, and inspired by a reading from the Bible interpreted by the leader of the service. Worship will often involve:

- **SINGING, MUSIC & PRAISE** - Including dancing and the raising of hands in praise

- **PRAYERS FOR HEALING** - Including people laying hands on another person to pray for God's blessing

- **SPEAKING IN TONGUES** - A language given by the Holy Spirit to communicate with God

- **A SERMON OR MESSAGE** - From the leader of the church outlining how the Bible applies to daily life

- **SPONTANEITY** - Other spontaneous acts of worship, including people sharing what they feel God is saying at that particular moment.

In the **QUAKER MOVEMENT**, services are conducted in silence, where someone speaks only if they feel they have received something to share from the Holy Spirit.

Christian worship, though practised differently, is based on the Bible and the teaching of the Church as sources of wisdom and authority and has the purpose of helping people to:

- **HONOUR GOD**

- **EVANGELISE** - Bring greater understanding of the nature of God the Trinity and his plans for the world

- **GROW** - In their faith

Worship, however practiced, plays a significant and meaningful part in helping Christians to live out their beliefs.

Comparison with Sikh worship

Like Christians, Sikhs can worship privately, as it is believed God is omnipresent. There are set prayers that a Sikh can recite, and these help Sikhs to feel that, although God is beyond description, he cares for humanity and people can spend time with him. Sikhs are encouraged to develop a regular pattern of worship in the home in order to build a relationship with God.

The purpose of private and public worship in **SIKHISM** is to focus on God and try to commit themselves to living a selfless, honest and good life.

Public worship takes place in the **GURDWARA**. Any competent Sikh, male or female, can lead worship, and it involves:

- **DRESSING APPROPRIATELY** - Taking off shoes and wearing head covering as a sign of respect

- **KIRTAN** - Singing hymns (Kirtan)

- **GURU GRANTH SAHIB** - Listening to the reading of the Guru Granth Sahib, the Sikh Scripture. This reading takes central place in worship, as Sikhs regard the Guru Granth Sahib as the supreme and final authority and source of wisdom; guru means "teacher". At the end of worship, the Guru Granth Sahib is covered and placed in a private room as a sign of respect

As part of worship, Sikhs celebrate a communal meal, known as the Langer, to which any member of the local community is welcome.

Although there are differences over many beliefs in Sikhism and Christianity, such as reincarnation and who Jesus is, there are patterns of worship, such as prayers, reading from the Scriptures and sharing a meal together, which are similar. In both religions, private and public worship is important for believers to grow in their knowledge of God.

The key emphasis in Sikhism is that worship becomes a part of everyday life. As God is present everywhere, Sikhs are encouraged to honour God by serving others, so that daily living can become worship.

THE ROLE OF THE SACRAMENTS IN THE CHRISTIAN LIFE

The sacraments play a significant role in the life and worship of most Christian churches, and many are practised regularly throughout the Church year. The sacraments, and particularly Baptism and the Eucharist, help Christians honour God and understand more of his nature, which is the core of Christian worship.

They also:

- **STRENGTHEN** - Help Christians to celebrate and grow in their faith

- **EMPHASISE** - Core beliefs

- **REMIND** - Christians of their involvement in the wider church community

The role and practice of the sacraments within the Roman Catholic tradition

Seven sacraments are practiced within the Roman Catholic and Orthodox traditions:

- **BAPTISM**

- **CONFIRMATION**

- **HOLY COMMUNIION**

- **CONFESSION**

- **MARRIAGE**

- **ORDINATION**

- **ANOINTING OF THE SICK**

The sacraments are:

> *"The life of the Catholic Church. Each sacrament is an outward sign of an inward grace ... each provides us with the life of God in our soul. In worship, we give to God that which we owe Him; in the sacraments, He gives us the graces necessary to live a truly human life."*

It can be seen from this quotation that sacraments are at the heart of Roman Catholic worship. The first three sacraments are known as sacraments of initiation, which welcome into the Church. The other sacraments mark very significant stages in the life of a believer, though only those who are called to the Priesthood receive the sacrament of Ordination.

The Liturgy of the Eucharist is the most important aspect of Roman Catholic worship, and takes place as the central part of The Mass. The participation in the Eucharist reminds the participants of the Church's core beliefs about the death and resurrection of Jesus, the forgiveness of sin, salvation, redemption and atonement.

The role and practice of the sacraments within the Anglican (Church of England) tradition

Article 25 of The 39 Articles states:

> *"There are two Sacraments ordained of Christ our Lord in the Gospel, that is to say, Baptism and the Supper of the Lord."*

Baptism and the Eucharist are central to **ANGLICAN** worship. These sacraments are believed to be signs of God's grace and help stimulate faith in a person, and strengthen the person who is already a Christian.

The reason that the Anglican tradition teaches that there are only 2 sacraments is:

- **NEW TESTAMENT** - Baptism and the Eucharist are based on a New Testament command of Jesus

- **NO COMMANDS** - The other 5 sacraments listed within the Roman Catholic tradition are seen as important rites, but there are no commands of Jesus to carry them out, only examples of them in the Bible

Therefore, the 1662 **COMMON BOOK OF PRAYER** states that only 2 sacraments are necessary to salvation.

The practice and role of Baptism and the Eucharist within different traditions

▸ Baptism

ROMAN CATHOLIC TRADITION	CHURCH OF ENGLAND TRADITION
Infant baptism is the usual way of welcoming a person into the life of the Church, though adult baptism sometimes takes place. The baptism is held at the font. This sacrament celebrates the possibility of new life that God has given through the death and resurrection of Jesus. Baptism represents "dying" of an old life (going under water) and rising to new life (coming out of the water).	Similar to the RC tradition. The baptism is sometimes called a christening. However, some non-CofE Protestant traditions do not baptise infants. They argue that it is such an important step that the person must be an adult to agree to be baptised, understand the core beliefs being emphasised, and make the promises to follow the way of Christ.
Because of the nature of the promises that are made by the parents and godparent/s during the baptism, one of the godparents who supports the family at the ceremony and who are encouraged to have a nurturing role in the child's life, has to be a baptised Catholic.	Every child should have no fewer than three godparents, at least two of the same sex as the child. Godparents must be baptised, but not necessarily in the CofE tradition.

Roman Catholic:

- The priest makes a sign of the cross on the baby's head to "claim" him or her for Christ
- Parents and godparents make baptismal promises based on the Apostles Creed and renounce evil on their own behalf and that of the child
- Oil is used to signify the child becoming a member of the Church and to represent the strengthening and courage of the Holy Spirit
- Water which has been blessed will be poured over the child's head
- The priest will say, "I baptise you [name] in the name of the Father, the Son and the Holy Spirit"
- A Baptismal candle will be lit from the Easter candle to symbolise the light of Christ
- An adult baptism is similar to an infant baptism, except that the adult being baptised makes the promises.

Church of England:

- The CofE service follows the same pattern.
- In both denominations, water is symbolic of the child being cleansed of original sin and given new life in Jesus.* Without water no life can grow and so baptism is the sign of new spiritual life.
- Baptism is a core practice within both traditions as it is the welcome into the church and is the crucial first step in the journey of faith.
- Most Christians in both traditions believe that being baptised is necessary to becoming a Christian. Other traditions believe baptism is a sign of faith, but does not give salvation to a person, as that is an adult decision based on acceptance of Christ.

* See the section on Christian beliefs for more information on 'original sin'.

▸ Holy Communion or Eucharist

ROMAN CATHOLIC TRADITION	CHURCH OF ENGLAND TRADITION
The instruction to celebrate the Eucharist is based on following Christ's instruction during the Last Supper (see Christian beliefs section) and St Paul's command to follow this practice in 1 Corinthians 11:23-24.	
The Bible and Church tradition are the two most important sources of wisdom and authority in Christianity and the reason most churches practice baptism and the Eucharist.	
Unlike the sacrament of baptism, there are quite a few differences between the way that the Holy Communion or Eucharist is understood in these two traditions.	
The most important part of RC worship. The Mass is separated into sections: <ul><li>The believer prays for forgiveness and the priest grants absolution (release from guilt or punishment)</li><li>Passages from the Bible are read</li><li>The Priest celebrates the Liturgy of the Eucharist</li><li>The Lord's Prayer is recited and the consecrated bread is received by the congregation</li></ul>	The Eucharist or Holy Communion or Lord's Supper follows a similar pattern.
Within the RC tradition, it is believed that, after consecration, the bread and wine, without changing their physical shape, actually become the body of Christ. This is called Transubstantiation. This is based on the words of Jesus when he shared the supper with his disciples and said, "Take, eat, this is my body … this is my blood." Christ's presence in the elements of bread and wine is called the Real Presence.	In the CofE tradition, it is also taught that Jesus is really present in the bread and wine. However, as a sacrament, the bread and wine remain "outward and visible signs of an inward grace", and do not actually transform into the body and blood of Christ. Although the bread and wine represent Christ's real spiritual presence, this is not the same as Transubstantiation, which the 39 Articles reject.
<ul><li>The beliefs that the Mass celebrates and reiterates are at the core of Christianity, as noted above. In this way, this sacrament helps to remind Christians of all denominations what is essential to faith and belief</li><li>The Mass is offered on a daily basis</li><li>It is compulsory for a Roman Catholic to attend Mass on a Sunday</li><li>Continuing to take part in the sacraments is essential to maintaining a person's salvation</li></ul>	<ul><li>The Church of England offers the Eucharist or Holy Communion on a weekly basis and some churches more frequently</li><li>Attendance at the Eucharist is not compulsory, but encouraged</li><li>Anglicans believe that "the Scriptures contain" all things necessary for salvation'. Baptism and the Eucharist are ways of receiving the grace of Christ and they demonstrate and confirm faith.</li></ul>

In complete contrast to the significant place that the two traditions above place on the sacraments, The Salvation Army, a Protestant denomination, states that the sacraments are not essential to salvation. It does not practice baptism or the Eucharist in any of its services, as it does not believe a specific service, rite or ceremony is needed for the grace of God to be present.

> *"The Salvation Army has never said it is wrong to use sacraments, nor does it deny that other Christians receive grace from God through using them. Rather, the Army believes that it is possible to live a holy life and receive the grace of God without the use of physical sacraments and that they should not be regarded as an essential part of becoming a Christian."*

THE NATURE AND PURPOSE OF PRAYER

Private and public prayer is a key part of Christian practice. Christians pray in order to:

- **EXPRESS THANKS** - To God for his goodness, love and blessing

- **CONFESS** - The things they have done wrong, and ask for God's forgiveness. This can be known as penitential prayer, when the Priest leads the congregation to privately confess their sins

- **NEEDS MET** - Bring their needs, the needs of others and the wider world to a loving Father

- **MAINTAIN & DEVELOP** - Their relationship with God though asking for the help of the Holy Spirit

- **UNDERSTANDING** - Try to understand what God wants them to do, and grow in Christian virtue, following the example of Jesus

- **LAMENT** - A lament is a passionate expression of grief, sorrow or regret, or even a complaint to God. There are many examples of this type of prayer in the Bible (for example, Psalm 22: 1-2 and Psalm 10:1)

There are also many different ways in which Christians pray, for example:

Prayer using liturgy

Many Christians are helped by the rhythm, structure and careful and thoughtful expression of the liturgy.

An example of this is when Christians are led through the Mass or Eucharist by the Priest and are asked to confess their sins in penitential prayer. In the Roman Catholic tradition, the congregation respond to the Priest's invitation to admit that they have not lived up to God's standards by saying:

> *"I confess to almighty God and to you, my brothers and sisters, that I have greatly sinned in my thoughts and in my words, in what I have done and in what I have failed to do, through my fault, through my grievous fault; therefore I ask blessed Mary ever-Virgin, all the Angels and Saints, and you, my brothers and sisters, to pray."*

Many other Christians confess their sins to God without using liturgy, but in their own words. Protestant churches do not believe in praying to the Virgin Mary or the Angels or Saints because they do not think this is what the Bible recommends in prayer. They believe prayers, inspired by the Holy Spirit, should be said directly to God.

Collect

Another type of prayer used by many Christians in a wide range of churches is a Collect, which simply means a short general prayer used as part of the liturgy. Anglican congregations are led through a collect for each Sunday, and there are different collects for the Christian festivals and seasons. An example of a collect is one that is said on Christmas Day at the end of Advent:

> *"Almighty God, you have given us your only-begotten Son to take our nature upon him and at this time to be born of a pure virgin: grant that we, who have been born again and made your children by adoption and grace, may be daily renewed by your Holy Spirit; through Jesus Christ our Lord."*

Praying in tongues

A very different type of prayer to the more formal examples listed above, is "praying in tongues", which was known in the Bible as glossolalia. Many Christians, particularly in the Pentecostal and Charismatic traditions, pray in private and public using this "language", which they believe has been given to them by God, and which they do not necessarily understand, unless someone interprets it for them. This is because they feel that there should be freedom in worship and prayer, and that set liturgy sometimes does not express what is on their heart and mind at that particular time, and only God can help them express that.

It is believed Jesus promised the gift of tongues to his followers. He said that, when the Holy Spirit comes, believers will, "drive out demons, speak in tongues … " (Mark 16:17)

There are examples of this in the New Testament. When Paul visited Ephesus, "he placed his hands on 12 men; the Holy Spirit came upon them and they spoke in tongues" (Acts 19:6)

Paul advises the church in Corinth that when they pray in tongues they should pray that someone should be able to interpret what they are saying (1 Corinthians 14:13)

Sincerity in Prayer

Jesus taught his followers how to pray in Matthew 6:5-14. He said that God is looking for sincerity in prayer. and outlined what is now known as the Lord's Prayer, which has been used for the past 2,000 years in Christian worship:

> *"Our Father in heaven, hallowed be your name.*
>
> *Your kingdom come, your will be done, on earth as it is in heaven.*
>
> *Give us this day our daily bread,*
>
> *and forgive us our debts, as we have also forgiven our debtors.*
>
> *Lead us not into temptation, but deliver us from evil.*
>
> *For if you forgive others their trespasses, your heavenly Father will also forgive you."*

Many Christians have found this an inspiring prayer and a source of authority, and use it regularly because:

- **STARTS WITH PRAISE** - It starts with praise to God and acknowledges him as a Father

- **ASKS FOR A PRESENCE** - Asks that God's will (or plan) take place on earth, which is what all Christians want as they believe this will be good and loving

- **PRAYS FOR SUSTENANCE** - Prays for daily supplies and provisions

- **ASKS FOR FORGIVENESS** - And recognises the need to forgive others

- **ASKS FOR GUIDANCE** - Asks for God to guide them away from evil and temptation

- **RECOGNISES FOREGIVENESS** - Recognises that they must forgive others if they want to receive God's forgiveness

Many Christians pray in private, sometimes using prayer beads or icons to help them focus. Others use sources of wisdom and authority such as the Bible, teaching from influential Christians or inspiring books to help them pray.

PILGRIMAGE

Although the tradition of pilgrimage is often seen to be stronger in the Catholic tradition, many Christians from different denominations develop their faith by making a special journey to a holy place. This is not the same as being a tourist. The journey has deep significance and meaning, and can often be quite difficult to make in terms of what is involved, cost and time. Pilgrimages are therefore often acts of sacrifice and part of worship.

The history of Christian pilgrimage

- **ROOTS IN JUDAISM** - The roots of the Christian faith are in Judaism. The Jewish people often made sacred journeys to celebrate important events in the Jewish faith. One such journey was the journey to Jerusalem to celebrate the Passover Festival, as recorded in Luke 2:41-43. It is recorded here that Jesus made the journey to Jerusalem when he was 12 years' old.

- **RETRACING JESUS' STEPS** - Early Christians retraced the steps Jesus took in the last week of his life, in one of the earliest examples of pilgrimage. Still today, Christians make a pilgrimage to Jerusalem to walk the Via Delarosa or the way of sorrow where Jesus walked on the way to where he was to die.

- **ANCIENT SITES OF SIGNIFICANCE** - In the 4th and 5th Century there is evidence of pilgrimages to Rome and places where Christian martyrs had been executed or appearances of the Virgin Mary were reported to have taken place.

- **MODERN SITES OF SIGNIFICANCE** - After Jerusalem fell into Muslim hands in the 7th Century, important sites in Europe became places of pilgrimage. A shrine to St James was established in Santiago de Compostela (northern Spain) in the 9th Century. This followed the legend that the body of St James had been found there.

Storytelling

Other important sites, such as: Lourdes, Walsingham and Canterbury have stories attached to them regarding

- **LOURDES** - Visions of Mary

- **WALSINGHAM** - Replicas of the house in Nazareth in which the Angel Gabriel announced the news of Jesus' birth

- **CANTERBURY** - Tombs of saints such as Thomas a Becket (Canterbury Cathedral) where Christians in the Middle Ages would visit hoping to receive forgiveness of sin, increase their chances of going to heaven, and healing from illness

The purposes of a pilgrimage

- **TO LEARN FROM PAST PILGRIMS** - To gain some connection with and learn from earlier pilgrims and the journey they made

- **TO GAIN GREATER UNDERSTANDING** - Of the place to which they are journeying, and why it has significance in the history of the Christian faith

- **TO FOCUS ON GOD** - To separate from the usual schedule of life in order to concentrate on God and develop their relationship with him through prayer on the pilgrimage

- **TO RENEW FAITH** - And gain spiritual strength for living the Christian life

- **TO FIND THEMSELVES** - To discover what God might be calling them to do in life

- **TO BE PART OF A COMMUNITY** - To join with, and learn from, other pilgrims in the world wide Christian community in order to strengthen their own faith and gain a greater and broader understanding of what following Jesus means

The nature of Pilgrimage

Walking the path of sorrow is specifically associated with the pilgrimage to Jerusalem. Other places of worship have specific tasks and actions associated with them, which enable the pilgrim to gain greater understanding of the place to which they have journeyed:

- **WALSINGHAM** - At Walsingham, Catholic and Protestant pilgrims will often walk to the Catholic Slipper Chapel and, in the town of Walsingham the Anglican Shrine of our Lady of Walsingham, praying along the journey. The focus of the pilgrimage is the incarnation of Christ and paying devotion to Mary; pilgrims can also drink holy water from the fountain near Slipper Chapel.

- **IONA** - A Christian community off the west coast of Scotland exists to remember and celebrate Celtic Christianity. In 563AD St Columba and 13 followers established a monastery on the island, and Christians of many denominations have made pilgrimages to the site since then. The emphasis during a pilgrimage to Iona today is on retreat and contemplation, prayer and renewal of faith, with the hope that pilgrims return ready to live out their faith in service to others.

- **TAIZE** - Each year, many thousands of pilgrims journey to Taize in central France, where a monastery was established in 1940. Taize has developed meaningful worship in which phrases are repeated several times to simple harmonies. This gives the pilgrim chance to contemplate the meaning of the words and renew their faith. Pilgrims can join with the monks in quiet worship in order to explore or rediscover the Christian faith.

The highpoint of many pilgrimages is sharing the Mass or participating in the Eucharist with other pilgrims from all over the world who have made the same spiritual journey. This celebrates the beliefs that join pilgrims together and give a sense of the worldwide Christian Church and community of believers.

Arguments Against Pilgrimage

Whilst pilgrimage is very important in some Christian traditions as it helps the believer develop their spirituality, reaffirm their beliefs and refocus their lives, some Christians, mainly within the Protestant tradition, suggest that it is not important in the 21st Century:

- **ESCAPE FROM LIFE** - Pilgrimage can act as an escape from life, and an attempt to locate God in one specific place. However, there is no need to take such a journey as the Holy Spirit is present everywhere to help people.

- **IDOLATRY** - Other Christians argue that the concentration on relics or particular shrines or saints can raise the possibility of idolatry - that is, the worship of things that are not God, or get in the way of God.

- **NO SPECIAL MERIT** - Some Christians are concerned that people might get the idea that God is impressed by the person who goes on a pilgrimage. They would argue that pilgrimages cannot gain God's favour or special merit.

However, a Catholic understanding of pilgrimage is not to try to win God's favour but to honour him and his saints by making a journey, to trace the path Jesus and/or the saints trod, and to renew commitment to him.

> *"Pilgrims are sojourners - travellers on a quest of faith. Each of us is invited to a path of renewal and redemption, following after Jesus Christ. This is the path of the pilgrim. Christians make pilgrimages to pray, to offer penance, and to be renewed in the Christian life. A journey to a holy place reminds us of our life's journey to eternity in heaven. Pilgrimages are journeys of prayer to a holy site. They are not always easy or convenient. But they surprise us with the goodness of God."*

CELEBRATIONS AND FESTIVALS

The Church divides the year into different seasons. These seasons follow what is called the **ROMAN RITE**, which goes back to around the 4th Century when the Roman Empire established Christianity as the state religion. After the Reformation when the Church of England broke away from Rome, this rite was still followed.

In these different seasons there are festivals which mark a significant occasion, or remember important saints. For different seasons churches will be decorated using different colours and the priest will wear different coloured robes. In the many churches that follow the pattern of the Church calendar, specific Bible readings, prayers and themes for preaching will be set for the different seasons.

The Church calendar is organised around two major times:

Advent & Christmas

Advent begins the **CHURCH YEAR**. The word Advent means **COMING** or **ARRIVAL** and is significant because it prepares to celebrate:

- **THE BIRTH OF CHRIST** - This is its primary focus

- **THE RETURN OF CHRIST** - It looks forward to the **SECOND ADVENT**, at the end of time. Because of this, the season is one which **LOOKS TO THE FUTURE**, as well as back to the birth of Christ 2,000 years ago

- **INCARNATION & GOD'S LOVE** - It reminds Christians of the core beliefs about the Incarnation and God's love in coming to earth as fully man and fully God

It helps Christians remember to always **LIVE IN PREPARATION** for the coming of Christ at the end of time. Advent is a season of preparation and expectation that reminds Christians to trust in Christ and pray for his love to come into a dark world, just like his love came when he was born on earth. This hope inspires Christians to think that he will come again to bring justice and hope.

It reminds Christians of the delivery of the Jewish people in the past, so links their faith to history. In **ISAIAH 9**, the writer says that:

> *"The people walking in darkness have seen a great light"*

and Christians take this light to mean the birth of Christ.

▶ Church Decoration

- **ADVENT** - Purple or violet; associated with humility and penance

- **CHRISTMAS** - White and gold; associated with joy and purity

- **EPIPHANY** - White and gold

This time celebrates the time of preparation for the coming of Christ, his birth and the arrival of the Three Kings.

Because of the nature of Advent, there is both gladness in the Church during this season, but also awareness that believers should be living in the right way when Christ comes.

In the **ORTHODOX CHURCH**, Advent is a time of fasting (going without food for periods of time) and repentance for sins.

▸ Advent Wreaths

In many churches an **ADVENT WREATH**, with four purple candles around the outside and one white candle on the inside, is used. The four are lit on each of the four Sundays of advent representing expectation, hope, joy and purity.

The middle candle is lit on Christmas Day and represents Christ, the Light of the World

The 4 candles can also represent:

- **THE PATRIARCHS** - Jewish leaders in the Old Testament

- **THE PROPHETS** - People in the Old Testament who said the Messiah would come

- **JOHN THE BAPTIST** - Who welcomed Jesus at the start of Jesus' ministry

- **THE VIRGIN MARY**

Specific prayers, Bible readings, and liturgy is used to help people properly prepare for the coming of Christ and all that his life means.

CHRISTMAS has only recently become a holiday, and for many Easter is the more important celebration in the Christian calendar. However, more people attend church at Christmas than at any other time of the year. The actual Christmas season in the Church starts on Christmas Eve and lasts until January 5th.

Within the Christian Church, the meaning of Christmas is that God steps into human existence and changes the world by giving people hope that light is always going to triumph over darkness, and that God is with us and knows what it is like to struggle as a human being. One name given to Christ is **IMMANUEL**, which means **GOD IS WITH US**. It also gives Christians chance to celebrate God's gift of salvation and to reflect on the meaning of peace and goodwill.

▸ Services

Christmas celebrates the **INCARNATION**, and the festival represents the beginning of the life and ministry of Jesus. Churches celebrate this season through:

- **NATIVITY SCENES** - Acting out the birth of Christ

- **SPECIAL SERVICES** - Such as a Midnight Mass held at the start of Christmas Day - the name Christmas comes from "Christ's Mass"

- **CAROLS & CHRISTINGLE** - Celebrations through carol services and making of things

- **FAMILY SERVICES** - On Christmas morning

- **EXCHANGING GIFTS** - To remember the gifts given by the wise men to Jesus

Lent & Easter

The most important Christian Festival is **EASTER**.

Christians prepare for Easter through the 40 days of **LENT**, where they remember the time Jesus spent fasting and praying in the wilderness. Starting on **ASH WEDNESDAY**, Christians take time to consider what they can do to more closely follow the example of Christ in the way they live. This is a day of reflection, during which ash is placed on a person's forehead to symbolise the dust that they are made of; this comes from the Jewish tradition of penance.

▸ Church Decoration

- **LENT** - Churches are decorated in purple or violet

- **HOLY WEEK** - Red: associated with passion and love

- **EASTER** - White

- **PENTECOST** - Red; associated with the fire of the Holy Spirit

▸ Festival Schedule

- **LENT** - Prepares people for Easter and runs from **ASH WEDNESDAY** to the Thursday of Holy Week (40 days not including the Sundays in those weeks). Christians may give up something during Lent and try to think about others in practical ways.

- **HOLY WEEK** - Remembers the events that happened to Jesus from **PALM SUNDAY** to the Saturday after **GOOD FRIDAY**

- **EASTERTIDE** - Celebrates the resurrection of Jesus; beginning on the eve of **EASTER SUNDAY** through the next 50 days until Pentecost Sunday

- **PENTECOST** - The seventh Sunday after Easter, celebrates the gift of the Holy Spirit

▸ Holy Week

In many churches on **PALM SUNDAY**, palm branches are carried in processions and small crosses made of palm leaves are carried. This symbolises the palms which people in Jerusalem waved when Jesus rode on a donkey.

The act of riding a donkey reminds Christians that Jesus is a humble king

The crosses are burned at the start of Lent the next year to provide ash for Ash Wednesday.

Entering **HOLY WEEK**, Christians think carefully about the suffering and passion of Jesus. On **MAUNDY THURSDAY**, Christians remember and celebrate the last meal Jesus had with his disciples before he was arrested, which was probably a Jewish Passover Meal. Christians remember the meal by sharing the Eucharist, and in some churches the priest washes the feet of the congregation following Jesus' example to love and serve others.

On **GOOD FRIDAY**, Christians remember the arrest, trial, crucifixion, suffering, death and burial of Jesus. The altar is sometimes covered in black. Services are held to allow people to try to understand the pain and passion of Jesus and this day is **DEEPLY MEANGINGFUL AND SIGNIFICANT TO CHRISTIANS**.

▸ Easter Saturday and Sunday

On **EASTER SATURDAY** a vigil is held after the sun has gone down to begin to celebrate the resurrection of Christ. In the Roman Catholic tradition, an Easter Vigil Mass takes place and baptisms are carried out. The Easter candle is lit as a sign of Christ the light of Christ.

For many, this is the highest point of the Church calendar, because it celebrates Christ's triumph over death

EASTER SUNDAY is a day of celebration across the world wide Christian Church. Christians celebrate this day at the end of Holy Week as the day in which God's promises were fulfilled and death, evil and sin were defeated by Christ's resurrection from the dead.

This belief is essential in Christianity

Many Protestant Christians gather at sunrise to celebrate the Lord's Day and his resurrection, and most churches celebrate by sharing the Mass or Eucharist, with many people attending who don't always go to church.

As a source of authority, Christians place great stress on the teaching of the Bible

In **1 CORINTHIANS 15:12-34**, St Paul outlines that the Christian faith simply makes no sense if Christ has not been raised from the dead. There would be no hope for anyone when they die if Christ had not defeated death. But if Christ has risen from the dead, then he has defeated the death brought into the world by Adam, the first human, and will give that new life to people who believe in him when they die.

For this reason, sometimes Christians call Christ **THE SECOND ADAM.**

Easter is a celebration of this new life given through the resurrection of Christ

THE FUTURE OF THE CHRISTIAN CHURCH

Following the ascension of Jesus, the movement that would become Christianity had 12 disciples (close followers of Jesus) and a number of other people who accepted Jesus' teaching; there are now estimated to be 2.2 billion Christians, and the global Church continues to grow.

Christians believe they should continue this growth and spread the news about Jesus by encouraging other people to become Christians. Telling other people about the Christian faith is called **EVANGELISM**.

Many Christians believe evangelism is an essential part of their faith because Jesus' last message following his resurrection was to:

> *"Go into all the world and preach the gospel to all creation. Whoever believes and is baptised will be saved, but whoever does not believe will be condemned"*

Mark 16:15-16

Because Jesus' words in the Bible are a source of authority, many Christians think it is a duty to spread the faith as commanded by Jesus. Christians believe:

- **LIVE AT PEACE** - Life with a relationship with God is the way to live at peace in a challenging world. Christians believe the story of God's love is good news and want to share it. Jesus said knowing him was living:

"Life to the full"

John 10:10

- **EVERYONE SHOULD LISTEN** - The message of the resurrection of Jesus, for example in John 20:1-22, is the truth and everyone needs to hear it, especially as Christians believe everyone will face God's judgement when they die.

- **PUT INTO PRACTICE** - It helps to develop and grow their own faith and test out their beliefs; it helps Christians put into practice what they hear at church and read in the Bible.

CHRISTIANS HELP THE CHURCH TO GROW IN A NUMBER OF WAYS

Missionary Work

Throughout its history, Christians have engaged in missionary work. This is where people have traditionally left their own land and preached the Gospel to people who have never heard it. The early Christians did this throughout the Middle East, Asia and Europe, and other examples include:

- **BILLY GRAHAM** - An American Baptist minister, who has preached to millions of people at various locations, including football stadiums, throughout the world. The Billy Graham institute estimate that 3.2 million people have "accepted Jesus as their personal saviour" through his preaching

- **DR JAMES HUDSON TAYLOR** - Travelling to China in 1854, learning several local dialects, establishing the **CHINA INLAND MISSION** and eventually building 125 schools. CIM sent over 800 missionaries, and 18,000 conversions to Christianity have been recorded through their work

- **AMY CARMICHAEL** - An Irish missionary who travelled to India in 1902 and opened an orphanage which helped to rescue young children from being used as prostitutes.

The last two stories above show that Christians not only feel that they should spread the story of Jesus by telling other people about him, but that they should demonstrate God's love in their actions as a way to attract people to Jesus.

Evangelism

- **HUMANITARIAN SUPPORT** - Many global Christian charities such as World Vision and The Salvation Army believe that part of fulfilling the instruction of Jesus to preach the Gospel is for people to see God's love in action through aid projects, disaster relief and humanitarian support.

- **ALPHA COURSE** - In the UK, the Alpha course, held over 10 evenings during which people are invited to explore the Christian faith, has seen 1.2 million people attend, and the idea has spread to 169 countries. Many people have become Christians as a result of this course.

- **LOCAL EVANGELISM** - On a local level, Christians evangelise in different ways, from hiring space in a Bristol night club called The Cube to renting a tent and offering guidance and healing at Glastonbury Festival, to running specific services aimed at those who are not familiar with church.

Whilst the global Christian Church is still growing, the Church in Great Britain has seen a steady decline in attendance, from 11.8% of the population in 1980, to 5% in 2015, with many Christians concerned about its future. Furthermore, other religions, such as Islam and Buddhism, are growing. Many Christians feel therefore that it is very important to evangelise in order to try to reverse this trend and see people become Christians, following Jesus' command.

THE LOCAL CHURCH, ITS ROLE AND IMPORTANCE

The local church is a very important source of support to Christians, as it is where they gain a sense of belonging and identity alongside other people who share the same beliefs, and where they receive teaching and help to enable them to live out those beliefs. The local church will be the place in which Christians worship together, grow and celebrate rites of passage in a supportive environment of friends and family. The global Church, referring to the worldwide Christian community, is expressed through the local church, which in some denominations is known as a parish church.

Community Service

Christians will try to live out their beliefs by serving others in the local community

- **REGULAR WORSHIP** - The people of the local church come together regularly in worship, and often meet in smaller groups for weekly Bible study where Christians can learn more about their faith and receive support and encouragement.

- **COMMUNITY PRAYERS** - The local church pray for each other and the spiritual and physical needs of the local community. Because the Priest, or leader, and people in the congregation are from the area, they know people who need help in their neighbourhood and what is happening and important in that local community.

- **COMMUNITY SERVICES** - The local parish church will offer services such as the Eucharist, baptism, weddings and funerals for people in the parish.

Community Support

The local parish church will offer a range of other things that help support the local community such as:

- **COUNSELLING AND ADVICE**

- **SUPPORT FOR FAMILIES** - Children's groups, after school clubs and family services

- **SUPPORT FOR THE ELDERLY**

- **SUPPORT FOR THE NEEDY** - Food banks and lunch clubs

- **FINANCIAL & SOCIAL SUPPORT** - Support for people who are struggling financially, socially and emotionally

- **EMOTIONAL SUPPORT** - When a community suffers a tragic event, the church is often the place where people express their grief and receive support, whether or not they go to that church regularly or have a Christian faith.

Often the physical building of the church in the middle of a town acts as a place where people visit from time to time, or at special times through the year; churches are normally accessible and open to all.

The local church does this because it is trying to show the love of God in the local setting in practical ways, following the example of Christ

Local Ecumenism

Another way in which the church fulfils an important role in the local community is by working together with other churches. This is called ecumenism and makes the Christian presence stronger and more effective.

Churches working together shows Christian unity. Despite some differences between the interpretations of the Bible, the core beliefs of Christianity are shared across denominations. At the end of his life on earth, Jesus prayed that, just as there is unity between God the Father and God the Son, there would be togetherness between Christians (John 17: 21).

Christians work together to help the outreach in the local area be more effective and coordinated. Christians want others to hear the good news of Jesus and demonstrate his love, so will bring together the resources of different local churches to work more effectively.

Churches Together In England published a document in 2016 which states that:

> *"The task … of serving and transforming communities, making new disciples and growing in holiness and worship … is too great for one church to do on its own - even if it has large numbers of people attending it - it is a task for the whole people of God. Working co-operatively is about the sharing of resources and gifts in a partnership. Unity speaks to a divided world"*

An example of local ecumenism is where a Local Ecumenical Partnership is agreed so that various churches in one location come together in mission and action. The Walting Valley Partnership is:

> *"A lively family of Christians living out God's love in the west of Milton Keynes"*

and involves the United Reformed, Methodist, Baptist and Church of England congregations in partnership. There are different styles of worship offered in the 5 churches, a school, and a range of community activities offered in the buildings each week.

To enable churches to work effectively in the local community, leadership is important as teaching from those in authority can help the congregation understand that reaching out in the community is important, as it follows the example of Jesus, shows the love of God and enables the church to grow.

These are core parts of the Church's mission and local leadership can help to fulfil that.

In **1 PETER 5:1-4**, the Bible says that the Priest or leader of the local church has responsibility to act like a shepherd to their congregation, leading them gently, diligently and in a way which honours God.

THE CHURCH IN THE WORLDWIDE COMMUNITY

Christians believe that the Church should play a role in the worldwide community because:

- **EVERYONE IS YOUR NEIGHBOUR** - Jesus taught that the greatest thing a person can do is to love God and love their neighbour. Christians believe that everyone is their neighbour (Mark 12:29-31).

- **EVERYONE SHOULD BE CARED FOR** - Jesus emphasised in the Parable of the Good Samaritan (Luke 10:25-37) that the right and good thing to do is to care for anyone in need, even supposed enemies

- **YOU WILL BE JUDGED ON WHAT YOU DO TO HELP OTHERS** - People will be judged on what they have done to help others, particularly the most vulnerable. In the Parable of the Sheep and Goats (Matthew 25:31-46), Jesus outlined that serving people who are in prison, or naked, or hungry and thirsty is a way of serving him, and God rewards those who love "the least of these" and punishes those who don't take the opportunity to help.

- **EVERYONE HAS A RIGHT TO JUSTICE & EQUALITY** - As everyone is made in the image of God, all people have a right to justice and equality

Therefore, Christians are taught and inspired to preach the Gospel, and to bring hope and reconciliation to people across the world.

In Christian teaching, showing the love of God means working to overcome any barriers of race or nationality, and involves getting involved in practical ways. This is demonstrated in 1 Corinthians 13, which emphasises how love should be the primary Christian quality rather than impressive words or actions that are not done out of love.

Practical examples of the Church bringing reconciliation include:

Archbishop Desmond Tutu

In 1995 Tutu led South Africa's Truth and Reconciliation Commission to help South Africans come to terms with its troubled past and racial segregation. The task of the commission was to deal truthfully with the deeds that had been carried out by the government between 1960 and 1994, and bring support to the victims. The main aim of the commission was to start to bring reconciliation between enemies, motivated by the teaching of Jesus to love one another. Archbishop Tutu said that:

> *"If it were not for faith, I am certain that lots of us would be hate-filled and bitter … but to speak of God, you must speak of your neighbour"*

The Tutu Foundation in the UK was set up in 2007 to "prevent and resolve conflict, to help people build peaceful communities" and, amongst other things, is working to bring peace between religions and establish good relationships between different groups in Northern Ireland.

The Evangelical Alliance

Following the Brexit vote in the UK in June 2016, the Evangelical Alliance, an organisation that represents thousands of Christians, responded to the increase in hate crimes by publishing a statement to encourage reconciliation:

> *"This is an opportunity for the Church to ask itself challenging questions: what does it mean to love our neighbours - meaning the neighbours in our streets and those across the nations of Europe? We should witness the peace of God to those who are distressed, and we should be actively working to be peacemakers. We have the ministry of reconciliation"*

Christian Aid

Many Christians and Christian organisations, such as World Vision, Food for the Hungry, The Salvation Army and Christian Aid believe that following Jesus and spreading his Gospel means getting involved in helping the world's most vulnerable people. Inspired by the Bible readings above, Christian charitable work is expressed across the world.

Christian Aid provides "urgent, practical and effective assistance where need is great, tackling the effects of poverty as well as its root causes", as it attempts to create a world where everyone can live a full life, free from poverty. It is supported by donations from a mixture of fundraising and government grants. During Christian Aid week, many Christians raise money for the organisation.

Formed in the 1940s to help European refugees, its work across the world now includes:

- **DISTRIBUTION** - Distributing insecticide-treated mosquito nets in hard to reach rural areas

- **PROMOTION** - Promoting safe sex practices and help people living with HIV receive critical health services

- **EDUCATION** - Providing training to farmers to help ensure good crop yields

- **PROTECTION** - Promoting and protecting the rights of women in areas where they have been excluded socially, economically and politically

- **REHABILITATION** - Rehabilitating former child soldiers back into their communities

Some Christians argue that charity work can be done equally well by atheists and Christian charity work sometimes get in the way of sharing the full message of Christ which is about believing in him. In this situation, some Christians feel that feeding a person without also inviting them to become a member of the Church and receive the sacraments is only doing half of what Jesus commanded his followers to do.

Other Christians, such as some monks and nuns, feel that they are called to be separate from the world and commit themselves to a life of prayer. In that way, they support the work of those who are carrying out acts of charity by asking for God's help and blessing on it.

THE PERSECUTED CHURCH

Throughout its history, Christians have been persecuted, with most of Jesus' disciples being killed and thousands of people throughout the last 2000 years suffering for following Jesus.

Violence

In figures published by Open Doors, a Christian organisation that supports persecuted Christians, each month:

- 322 Christians are killed for their faith

- 214 churches and Christian properties are destroyed

- 772 forms of violence are committed against Christians

Persecution

Christians in more than 60 countries face persecution from their governments or neighbours simply because of their belief in Jesus Christ, with some countries banning Christian belief entirely.

Persecution happens because:

- **POLITICAL CONTROL** - Governments try to seek control of all religious thought and expression; loyalty should be to the State (North Korea) and not to God

- **MINORITY GROUPS** - Are seen as preaching a message against the official religion in the country (Saudi Arabia)

- **NO HUMAN RIGHTS** - Some countries do not allow basic human rights, such as the freedom of thought and religion

Suffering

The work of Open Doors is motivated by the Christian belief that the Church is like a "body" and if one part suffers, the whole body suffers with it. And Psalm 82:3 which says that people should:

> *"Stand up for those who are weak. See to it that those who are beaten down are treated fairly."*

Hebrews 13:3 also inspires Christians to:

> *"Remember those in prison as if you were their fellow prisoners, and those who are mistreated as if you yourselves were suffering."*

Before Jesus died he said that Christians would face trouble in this world, but they know he understands what suffering is like as he was tortured and killed. Christians who are being persecuted are also comforted by the words of Jesus in Matthew 5:10-12:

"Blessed are those who are persecuted because of righteousness, for theirs is the kingdom of heaven. Blessed are you when people insult you, persecute you and falsely say all kinds of evil against you because of me. Rejoice and be glad, because great is your reward in heaven, for in the same way they persecuted the prophets who were before you."

NEED MORE HELP ON LIVING THE CHRISTIAN LIFE?

Use your phone to scan this QR code

Matters of Life and Death

KEYWORDS

- **ABORTION** - The deliberate termination of a pregnancy

- **ANIMAL RIGHTS** - The rights of animals to be treated well and live free from cruelty, exploitation or abuse

- **ATHEIST** - A person who does not believe that God or Gods exist

- **ATHEISTIC EVOLUTION** - Life emerged through the natural evolutionary process without being started or directed by any God/s

- **BIG BANG THEORY** - Theory concerning the beginning of the universe approximately 13.7 billion years ago

- **CONCEPTION** - The fertilisation of an ovum by a sperm; the inception of pregnancy

- **EUTHANASIA** - The painless killing of someone suffering from a painful disease

- **ENVIRONMENT** - The surroundings in which plants, animals and humans live and on which they depend

- **EVOLUTION** - The process by which living organisms are believed to have developed from earlier forms

- **HOSPICE** - A home or hospital caring for the terminally ill

- **HUMANAE VITAE** - 1968 document from the Pope guiding Roman Catholics about family life and procreation

- **HUMANIST** - Someone who is particularly concerned about the welfare of other humans, believing that people are basically good without the need for God or religion

- **MAGESTRIUM** - The teaching authority of the Roman Catholic Church, especially as carried out by Bishops and the Pope

- **PARANORMAL** - Things that seem to be beyond normal explanation that are thought to have spiritual causes, such as ghosts

- **POLLUTION** - The contamination of the environment by substances that are harmful to living organisms

- **PRO-CHOICE** - Supporting the right of a woman to choose whether or not to have an abortion

- **PRO-LIFE** - A position opposed to abortion and supporting the life of the unborn

- **RESURRECTION** - Jesus rising from the dead; overcoming death

- **SANCTITY OF LIFE** - The belief that life is holy and belongs to God

- **SENTIENT** - Able to sense or feel things

- **SITUATION ETHICS** - A method of trying to do the most loving thing in each situation

- **THEISTIC EVOLUTION** - The belief that evolution was started and directed by God to bring human life into existence

- **UTILITARIANISM** - Ethical theory in which the right thing to do is that which maximises happiness and minimises pain

THE ORIGINS AND VALUE OF THE UNIVERSE

The most widely held scientific theory concerning the origins of the universe is the **BIG BANG THEORY**. The theory states that approximately 13.7 billion years ago all the matter of the universe was compressed into a single point of infinite density, which expanded or inflated ('the Big Bang'), causing matter to move away from the initial point. Eventually, over billions of years and after cooling and the effects of gravity, stars and planets were formed, including our own.

As difficult as it is for us to understand, the Big Bang did not appear in space and time, but was the beginning of space and time. Many scientists think that there was no "before" the Big Bang - no space or time, but nothing.

Evidence for the Big Bang Theory

Scientists have discovered that galaxies are moving away from us at speeds consistent with the initial Big Bang or expansion. **EDWIN HUBBLE'S** work in the 1920's work proposed an expanding universe, arguing that if the universe is expanding today it must have been smaller in the past.

Linked to the above is what is called the **REDSHIFT EFFECT**. Redshift is one way scientists use to tell the distance of any object that is far away in the universe:

- **BLUE APPROACH** - Objects, like stars, that are approaching us, will be at the blue end of the light spectrum

- **RED FADE** - Objects that are moving away from us will be at the red end of the spectrum. Astronomers have discovered that the further from us a star is, the more its light is red-shifted, meaning that galaxies are moving away.

This provides evidence that the universe is expanding in the way that the Big Bang theory suggests.

If the point of singularity which led to the Big Bang was infinitely hot, we should be able to find some left over of this heat in the universe. Scientists have been able to detect this. It is called **COSMIC MICROWAVE BACKGROUND RADIATION**.

The discovery of the Big Bang and the work of Georges Lemaître

In the 1920's and 30's Catholic priest **GEORGE LEMAITRE** observed red shift and proposed that the universe was expanding. Although he did not call his theory the Big Bang, Lemaître argued that this expansion of space must have derived from an initial **MOMENT OF CREATION**, which was called the **PRIMEVAL ATOM** or the **COSMIC EGG**.

Unlike many scientists at the time, Lemaître argued that the universe had a beginning, which he described as a:

> "*Burst of fireworks, comparing galaxies to the burning embers spreading out in a growing sphere from the centre of the burst. He believed this burst was the beginning of time, taking place on a 'day without yesterday.'*"

The idea that the expansion of the universe is accelerating, as first proposed by Lemaître, was confirmed by later discoveries by the **HUBBLE TELESCOPE** in the 1990's. Other findings, such as Cosmic Microwave Background radiation, have confirmed parts of Lemaître's work.

However, although Lemaître was a priest, he was keen to make a distinction between how scientific findings are investigated and the search for God:

- **INDEPENDENT** - He opposed the Church using scientific theories to support theological or faith positions, as he wanted the science to be judged as a scientific theory and not as something that did or did not support the existence of God.

- **PHILOSOPHICAL** - Lemaître was accused of denying the book of Genesis. He admitted that people found it easier to believe that time existed before the beginning of the universe, but said that was impossible. He argued that the question of whether there was something before the universe was a **PHILOSOPHICAL QUESTION**, which could not be settled by astronomical considerations.

- **NO CONFLICT** - Lemaître did not believe God could be reduced to a scientific hypothesis. He argued that science and religion are not in conflict, but are different and complimentary routes to truth, one theological, and one natural.

Christian responses to the theory of the Big Bang

▸ Creationism

Some Christians reject the theory of the Big Bang entirely. This position is called **CREATIONISM** and argues that:

- **BELIEVE IN THE BIBLE** - The Bible is all that is needed for the correct account of how the universe began. It was created in six 24-hour days as Genesis says, because God's word is literally true.

- **APPARENT AGE THEORY** - The data suggesting the universe is 13.7 billion years old can be accounted for by God creating a world that looked old to its first human inhabitants. This theory is known as the Apparent Age theory and suggests that things like developed ecosystems necessary for life appeared to be mature to Adam but were only just created.

- **FOSSILS ARE FROM NOAH'S FLOOD** - The story in Genesis 5 of the flood in which God saves Noah's family on an ark explains how fossils and strata were laid down quickly. Scientists who already believe in an old earth and evolution have incorrectly recorded the laying down of fossils and strata as taking place over a long period of time.

▸ Intelligent Design

Some Christians argue that "big bangs" normally cause destruction and chaos, not the life and order that can be seen in the universe today. This points to evidence of **INTELLIGENT DESIGN**:

- **UNLIKELY BEGINNING** - It is infinitely unlikely that this universe would ever come to exist as a result of blind chance or a big bang that had to be precisely right to produce life

- **WHO DESIGNED IT?** - So much design in the universe suggests an Intelligent Designer

- **IRREDUCIBLE COMPLEXITY** - So many intricate things fit together - they are **IRREDUCIBLY COMPLEX** - and could not have just arrived little by little, as unguided evolution suggests. The whole universe needs each part to be present at the same time for it to work.

▸ Science & Religion

Other Christians argue that science and religion are compatible:

- **NO CONTRADICTION** - There is no contradiction between believing in the Bible and science, as long as the Bible is not read literally or as a science text book, which was not the intention of the writers

- **NO DISAGREEMENT** - The general pattern of creation, such as light, then life etc., as outlined in the Genesis account, does not disagree with the Big Bang and the eventual formation of life

- **NEEDS A CREATOR & DESIGNER** - Laws of science, such as gravity and the precise measurement of it present in the Big Bang, plus exactly the right conditions on earth to form life, as well as the chemical and biological structures that enable life to exist, suggest the need for a wise and powerful God as creator and designer.

- **SUPPORTS GENESIS** - The Big Bang does suggest that the universe had a beginning and was made from nothing. Many Christians believe this does not contradict Genesis 1:1, which supports both of these ideas

- **SUPPORTS NATURAL PHENOMENA** - Science is good for a type of truth that explains natural phenomena, but has no way of proving or disproving God. Science and religion can work together to produce **PHYSICAL AND METAPHYSICAL TRUTHS**.

The value of the universe

Because Christians believe that God is the creator of the entire universe it is **VALUABLE**. It did not happen by chance, and is not a commodity for people to abuse but the work of a wise, loving and good creator.

This means that:

- **RESPONSIBLITY FOR THE PLANET** - Humanity has a responsibility to take care of it, with respect and responsibility. As the universe is a gift, humans should value it

- **NO RIGHT TO EXPLOITATION** - Humanity should not exploit the earth as if they own it and can do whatever they like with it

- **STEWARDSHIP** - People should act wisely with the limited resources of the earth, treating the environment, including animals and plants, with due value

- **ANCESTRAL** - Each generation should be aware that they need to pass the world on to others. In **LUKE 19:11-26**, Jesus taught that there is a responsibility to make the best and most wise use of gifts that one has been given.

The earth is a valuable gift from God for which we should care, but Christians believe that with this privilege comes responsibility. Christians also believe that when people are judged by God, all of our actions and behaviours, including our attitude to the gift of the earth, will be taken in to account.

Modern interpretations of the teaching in Genesis 1:26

- **DEPENDENCE ON THE NATURAL WORLD** - "Ruling" over the earth as the most **SENTIENT** creature must take into account our dependence on the natural world and ecosystems

- **RESOURCES ARE FINITE** - Exploitation of the world will be harmful for humanity and other life forms, and not value the gift God has entrusted to us. The earth should never be treated as a commodity

- **PRESERVE FOR THE FUTURE** - The way in which we fulfil our responsibility for the earth must reflect that we are **MADE IN THE IMAGE OF GOD**, as the next verse, Genesis 1:27, says. This involves working with **COMPASSION** to ensure that what is produced from the earth is shared fairly, and **WISELY**, so that the earth is not destroyed for **FUTURE GENERATIONS**.

THE SANCTITY OF LIFE

Christians believe that life is sacred, meaning it is holy and belongs to God

This is because in Genesis the creation of human life is described in the following way:

- **MADE IN THE IMAGE OF GOD** - All life is created by God but, uniquely, humanity is made in the image of God - **GENESIS 1:27**. Some Christians interpret this as meaning that humans are able to share, to a degree, some of the characteristics of God, such as compassion, and that they have a moral sense. It also means that humans can have a relationship with God.

- **HUMANITY COMPLETES CREATION** - In **GENESIS 1** God describes everything that he has created as good, which gives value to all living things. However, after finalising his work with the creation of human beings, he describes the creation as "very good", which Christians interpret as meaning that humanity completes creation and God's plan for the earth.

- **HUMANS ARE SACRED** - In **GENESIS 2:7** God, again uniquely, breathes his spirit into Adam, the first human. This means that humans are not just physical creatures, but have something of God in them, meaning that they are sacred.

The sections from Genesis outlined above are interpreted by Christians as meaning that humans alone have a soul, which gives humans unique status as being able to know and relate to a holy God.

Other support in the Bible for the sanctity of life:

▸ **Psalm 139**

- Humans are known by God before they were born, and formed by him in the womb

- The creation of humans is wonderful (literally, full of wonder)

- God thinks about human beings and knows them intimately

▸ Jeremiah 1:5

God says, "before I formed you in the womb, I knew you", which indicates that God has knowledge of us from conception. Some Christians interpret this as meaning humans have a soul at the moment of conception.

John 1: 14 says:

"The Word (God) became human and made his home among us. He was full of unfailing love and faithfulness. And we have seen his glory, the glory of the Father's one and only Son."

Christians believe that the sanctity of life is demonstrated most fully by God coming to earth as human in the form of Jesus. Because an all-mighty God has stepped into human life, 'putting skin on', human life is seen as valuable, sacred and holy.

▸ 1 Corinthians 6:19-20

St. Paul writes that the body is "the temple of the Holy Spirit who lives in you", which means that life is sacred.

The teaching that life is holy and sacred is very important to Christians today because:

- **EVERY LIFE IS SACRED/VALUABLE** - Belief in the sanctity of life gives intrinsic value to human life. This means life is valuable no matter what people do or what capacity they have; every life is valuable because every life is sacred.

- **GOD HAS A PLAN FOR EVERY LIFE** - It gives Christians a sense that God cares intimately for human life, and that he has a plan for every life.

- **IT GIVES GUIDANCE** - It helps to inform Christians that they should treat all people with respect and care.

- **IT SHAPES ETHICAL VIEWS** - The belief that human life is sacred and that every life has intrinsic dignity shapes Christian views on a range of ethical issues including abortion, suicide, euthanasia, the treatment of the body, genetic engineering, warfare, the taking of life, and capital punishment.

- **IT HAS AN AFTERLIFE** - It means that humans are not viewed as physical only, but have a soul that God has breathed into them, and which continues after death.

- **YOUR BODY IS A TEMPLE** - Many Christians are influenced by the teaching that life is sacred so will not smoke or drink, or take drugs, and honour God's gift carefully with their attitude towards sexual relations and the use of the body.

NON-RELIGIOUS EXPLANATIONS OF LIFE AND CHRISTIAN RESPONSES

Prominent evolutionary biologist and atheist, Professor **RICHARD DAWKINS**, does not agree that God created life or gave it its value. He also rejects the idea that humans have a soul.

In Out of Eden, Dawkins writes that,

"There is no spirit-driven life force, no throbbing, heaving, pullulating, protoplasmic, mystic jelly. Life is just bytes and bytes of digital information."

River Out of Eden

Dawkins and many scientists argue that human life is a result of a long evolutionary chain, where random genetic mutations have enabled certain life forms to exist in a harsh, unsympathetic and unguided process described as the **SURVIVAL OF THE FITTEST**. There is no God-created purpose to life, and human life is not "sacred", though it is special in a sense as humans are the most sentient of all known species.

Dawkins argues that:

"We are survival machines - robot vehicles blindly programmed to preserve the selfish molecules known as genes."

The Selfish Gene

The idea that life started from nothing is, according to Dawkins, "a staggeringly beautiful thing" which doesn't require being, "cluttered up with something so messy as a God."

The view of many scientists who are also atheists is that human life is simply the result of the earth being formed from the Big Bang, and ending up at the right distance from a source of energy, the sun, from which life could start to evolve.

For many people who do not accept religious explanations for the origins of life, humanity can still find value and meaning:

- **JEAN-PAUL SATRE -** Argued that all meaning and purpose starts with the individual getting rid of the idea that there is any special "essence" or bigger picture to life. We should simply use our freedom to make a choice, and when we do, the thing we choose becomes valuable and meaningful to us. So, if we freely choose to get married, that becomes valuable, but there is nothing of intrinsic value, such as life itself. (See section above for how this contrasts with Christian views about the sanctity of life giving humans intrinsic value)

- **CHAPLAIN GREG EPSTEIN** - As a Humanist, he argues that it is perfectly possible to find value in life without God, suggesting that, through the use of reason, humanity is able to live in a compassionate way and treat people with dignity without being told to do so by God.

Many atheists, as seen above, argue that the belief in the Bible and its statements on the origins and value of life are **INCOMPATIBLE** with scientific and non-religious explanations for life. However, a number of scientists argue that the value placed in life by God does not contradict their faith.

Many Christians believe it is possible to believe that human life was created by God through the process of evolution, so that life is still sacred

They do not agree with the idea that being a scientist implies being an atheist.

Many Roman Catholics and Protestant Churches who do not hold literal interpretations of the Bible teach that the theory of evolution, and the survival of the fittest, are **COMPATIBLE** with Christian belief in a God who creates life.

Christian Responses to Evolutionary Theory

"Theistic evolutionists argue that evolution is scientifically supported and well-founded, but maintain that evolution takes place only by God's will; while evolution could be an indirect process of creation, humanity is ultimately a direct creation of God"

- **POPE FRANCIS** - He said, in 2014, that there is no contradiction between God and evolution. Evolution requires, "the creation of beings that evolve", and the Big Bang, "does not contradict the intervention of the divine creator but, rather, requires it."

- **PROFESSOR ALISTER MCGRATH** - Holding a Doctorate in Science and another in Theology, sees no contradiction in holding together the belief in the amazing success of science, and belief in a God who creates the world. He suggests that the Christian faith generates moral values and ideas which, "give moral meaning and dignity to our existence."

Christian responses argue that evolution and the survival of the fittest is the way human life came about, but this alone does not explain the value of human life, which is given by God

In 2009, an important document produced by the Church of England Diocese of Manchester discussed religion, science, evolution and the origins and value of life. It outlined that:

- **CHRISTIANS SHOULD ALWAYS QUESTION** - The Christian faith does not require people to abandon their reason. In fact, Scripture asks some very "sharp questions" about God and the universe

- **INNACURATE VIEW OF CHRISTIANITY** - People have been persuaded by answers provided by Professor Dawkins and others that actually put forward an incomplete and historically inaccurate view of Christianity

- **A BALANCE OF VIEWS** - Christians need to challenge the "omnipotence" of science and reject the view that Christianity equals a rejection of scientific evidence

- **CHRISTIANITY OFFERS MORE** - Christianity has a significant role in confirming the dignity and value of human beings. In the era of technological advance, and issues such as human exploitation of the planet, Christianity can draw on ethical and moral traditions to help humanity shape its response. In areas such as healthcare, it is now acknowledged that spiritual wellbeing is essential and can aid physical recovery.

- **SEARCH FOR ANSWERS** - The scientific search is also one that looks for answers to ultimate questions about human existence. We want to understand the universe because we want to understand our place in it and we study the human genome because we are "fearfully and wonderfully made" (Psalm 139)

- **COLLABORATIVE NOT CONTRADICTORY** - "Collaboration between religion and science is mutually beneficial; and not contradictory. Such a relationship provides people with 'the tools to live in and learn from God's creation.'"

The responses given above to the scientific and non-religious explanations about the origins and value of life are important to Christians today. They demonstrate that:

- **SCIENCE IS NOT DESTRUCTIVE** - Scientific theories such as evolution do not destroy belief in God's role in the creation of humans. Theistic evolutionists believe that evolution is guided by God and part of his plan for humanity. This still gives life intrinsic value, meaning, dignity and purpose.

- **INTRINSIC DIGNITY** - There is a real need for science and religion to work together in challenging times. The Christian belief that humans have an intrinsic dignity because of the sanctity of life is an important consideration when discussing issues such as immigration, climate change, warfare, advances in genetic engineering and other moral issues. These require both knowledge of science and a clear view of the value and dignity of human beings.

THE SANCTITY OF LIFE AND ABORTION

Abortion is the deliberate termination of a pregnancy and in the UK must be performed in a hospital or specialist licensed clinic. It is legal in the UK up to 24 weeks if two doctors agree on one of the following conditions:

- **THE MOTHER'S LIFE IS AT RISK**

- **THE MOTHER'S PHYSICAL OR MENTAL HEALTH IS AT RISK**

- **THE CHILD MIGHT BE BORN SEVERELY HANDICAPPED**

- **THERE IS A RISK TO THE HEALTH OF THE MOTHER'S EXISTING CHILDREN**

After 24 weeks abortion is allowed if there is a substantial risk to the women's life or foetal abnormalities.

Abortion is a controversial ethical issue for various reasons:

- **WHEN DOES LIFE BEGIN?** - There is disagreement about when life begins. If the foetus is regarded as a human life, and taking human life in all circumstances is wrong, then abortion will be regarded as wrong. However, if it is believed that the foetus is not yet a human life, abortion might not be seen as wrong.

- **WHOSE RIGHTS ARE MORE IMPORTANT?** - The second issue is whose rights - the mother's or the baby's - should take priority. Even if it is thought that life has begun in the womb, but continuing the pregnancy is going to cause harm to the mother, or the baby will be born with severe abnormalities, some might regard the choice of abortion as the lesser of two evils.

- **WHOSE LIFE IS IT ANYWAY?** - Within Christianity, there is debate over the issue of abortion and what rights a person has to make life and death decisions, such as in the case of abortion. If all life belongs to God, do humans have the right to make the decision to allow an abortion?

- **CONFLICTS WITH SANCTITY OF LIFE?** - Within Christianity, there is a debate about whether life should be preserved at all costs, and if the quality of life as well as the sanctity of life has to be taken into consideration.

The belief that life is valued and sacred because it belongs to God has implications for Christians for the issue of abortion.

Christian pro-life views

The Roman Catholic Church and Christians in other denominations, teach that **LIFE BEGINS AT CONCEPTION**. At that moment, life has begun and therefore any act that purposely destroys that is **MURDER**. The deliberate ending of the life in the womb is going against God's plan, which is for pregnancy to be completed once conception has taken place. Every human being has the right to the life that God has given.

This view is based on the principle of the **SANCTITY OF LIFE**:

- **GENESIS 1:27 -** Humans are made in the **IMAGE OF GOD** and therefore made to have a relationship with him

- **1 CORINTHIANS 6:19** - The human body is a **TEMPLE OF THE HOLY SPIRIT**. The Bible says that, "you are not your own", which means that life belongs to God

- **EXODUS 20:13** - Humans are not allowed to take life, as this is murder

Further teaching in the Bible, a major source of authority, particularly within the Protestant and Evangelical Churches, includes:

- **JEREMIAH 1:5** - God says, "before I formed you in the womb, I knew you"

- **PSALM 139** - God is said to know a person in the womb:

  "For you created my inmost being; you knit me together in my mother's womb.

  I praise you because I am fearfully and wonderfully made;
  your works are wonderful, I know that full well.

  My frame was not hidden from you when I was made in the secret place, when I was woven together in the depths of the earth.

Your eyes saw my unformed body; all the days ordained for me were written in your book before one of them came to be."

The major **SOURCE OF AUTHORITY** for the Roman Catholic Church is the **MAGISTERIUM** which is the teaching of the Pope and the Bishops. The Magisterium protects the word of the Bible and the teaching of Christ. In **HUMANAE VITAE**, the Roman Catholic tradition repeats its stance against abortion in every circumstance by stating that:

"Direct abortion, even for therapeutic reasons, is to be absolutely excluded."

In response to the argument that it is sometimes the lesser evil to allow an abortion to take place in the case that the baby will be severely disabled, or the pregnancy is a result of rape, the Roman Catholic Church teaches that:

"It is never lawful, even for the gravest reasons, to do evil that good may come out of it - in other words, to intend directly something which of its very nature contradicts the moral order [eg abortion] … even though the intention is to protect or promote the welfare of an individual, of a family or society in general."

The document reminds Catholics that there are, "certain limits, beyond which it is wrong to go, to the power of [men and women] over their own bodies." In the Catechism of the Catholic Church, which is a summary of official Church teaching, Catholics are reminded that:

"God alone in the Lord of life … no one under any circumstances claim for himself the right directly to destroy an innocent human being."

For the above reasons the Roman Catholic and conservative Evangelical traditions oppose abortion under any circumstances

Other Christian responses

▸ Churches

The **CHURCH OF ENGLAND** and the **METHODIST CHURCH** also believe in the principle of the sanctity of life.

However, there are certain circumstances where abortion might be the lesser of two evils, such as:

- **RAPE** - Where the pregnancy is a result of rape

- **DISABILITY** - The baby is likely to be born severely handicapped or not survive outside the womb

- **LIFE AT RISK** - The mother's life is at risk

In these circumstances, the Church of England teaches that it would in fact be evil to withdraw compassion, though it recognises, as does the Methodist Church, that abortion is not a "good" thing, but still the lesser of two evils.

As can be seen in the second point above, some Christians argue that the **QUALITY OF LIFE** must be taken into consideration, alongside the **SANCTITY OF LIFE**. In this position, life is still regarded as precious and a gift of God, but if that life is going to be severely incapacitated, with such things as repeated organ failure, or face a life of pain, then abortion might be the more **COMPASSIONATE** response. Advances in medicine mean it is possible to identify foetal abnormalities more quickly, and therefore allow abortion to take place earlier in the pregnancy, which can reduce the chance of side effects for the woman.

Christians who take this position argue that:

- **BE COMPASSIONATE** - Jesus taught his followers to be compassionate and loving, and in some situations, such as rape, the kind thing to do is to allow an abortion.

- **VIABILITY** - Life might not begin at conception, but later in the pregnancy, at such stages as when the baby can respond to stimuli, or when the baby could survive outside the womb (this is called viability). In such cases, an early abortion could be allowed without breaking the principle of the sanctity of life

▸ Situation Ethics

Each situation is judged on its merits. There are no rules which say that "abortion is always wrong" or, "the sanctity of life must always be preferred".

The guiding principle of this ethical theory is "what action is the most loving for those involved?". This love known as **AGAPE** love, which is a love that is always looking to serve the needs of others, and the same as God's love for each person. It is argued that this principle was the one Jesus lived by.

If the two points above are taken into consideration, then a person who follows Situation Ethics will carefully take account of each situation and the people involved, and try to look for the action that will be the most loving. On a case by case basis, this could include abortion.

This is entirely against Roman Catholic teaching, as it is seen as:

- **DISMISSIVE** - Disregarding the principle of the sanctity of life that applies in all situations and to all people

- **TOO EMPOWERING** - Putting too much power into human hands; power that belongs to God

- **AGAINST THE TESTAMENTS** - Looking for ways to use Jesus' teaching to fit human actions, rather than the other way round. Roman Catholics argue that Jesus did not abandon the moral commands in the Old Testament, but said that they should be applied in love. This includes the idea that the New Testament upholds the principle of the sanctity of life.

- **TOO SUBJECTIVE** - As it allows for love to be interpreted in ways which go against the dignity of the human being

▸ Humanists

Humanist positions on abortion would be closer to those found in Situation Ethics than Church positions, though they would not make any reference to a God-like agape love.

Although there is not one humanist or atheist position, many who believe that there is no God and that reason, not religion, is the best way to approach situations, would take a **PRO-CHOICE** stance. However, there would also be consideration of the rights and dignity of the life in the womb.

The British Humanist notes that:

"Abortion is an issue that demonstrated the difficulties of rigid rules in moral decision making. So in thinking about abortion a humanist would consider the evidence, the probable consequences, and the rights and wishes of everyone involved, trying to find the kindest course of action or the one that would do the least harm."

After discussing a range of positions, the BHA rejects religious views because:

- **SANCTITY OF LIFE UNHELPFUL** - The principle of the sanctity of life is unhelpful, especially if one has to choose between the child and the mother

- **INVALID ARGUMENTS** - People "play God" all the time in medical interventions so the argument that we are playing God on abortion is not valid

It concludes that,

"There is not one, correct humanist view on abortion. However, humanists <u>tend</u> to converge on a liberal, 'pro-choice' stance ...

Humanists do not think that all life is 'sacred' but do respect life ...

Humanists do not tend to think that - based on scientific evidence about foetal development - a foetus does not become a person, with its own feelings and rights, until well after conception.

Because humanists take happiness and suffering as foremost moral considerations, quality of life will often trump the preservation of life at all costs, if the two come in to conflict."

‣ Atheism

As atheism is not an organised movement as such, there are a **WIDE RANGE OF VIEWS** held:

- **PRO-CHOICE POSITION** - Some atheists maintain a pro-choice position as it respects the autonomy of the woman who is the mature life in the decision-making process

- **FLEXIBLE VIABILITY** - Other atheists, whilst not agreeing with the idea of the sanctity of life, make decisions about abortion based on when life begins, and opinion is divided about this

- **PRO-CHOICE NOT PRO-ABORTION** - Some atheists hold the position of being pro-choice without being pro-abortion. This position states that whilst the choice of whether to have an abortion or not should be the mother's, and not based on any consideration that the life she is carrying is sacred or belongs to God, it is important to consider the rights of the life, including future rights

- **CHRISTOPHER HITCHINS** - Atheist Christopher Hitchins considered the occupant of the womb, as a **CANDIDATE MEMBER OF SOCIETY** and that the, "unborn entity has a right on its side"

- **KRUSZELNICKI** - President of Pro-Life Humanists, writes to support finding real choices for women, instead of just the choice between continuing pregnancy and having an abortion. She notes that:

"I'm an atheist and I'm pro-life because some choices are wrong, violent, and unjust - and I want to do whatever I can to make abortion both unthinkable and unnecessary."

LIFE AFTER DEATH

Resurrection

Because of the **RESURRECTION OF JESUS** and his teaching concerning life after death, and the consistent theme of life after death in the Bible, Christians believe that **DEATH IS NOT THE END**, and this is one of the **CORE BELIEFS OF CHRISTIANITY**. However, there are different views about what happens after death and the nature of that life.

Many Christians, particularly from the Evangelical traditions, believe in the **RESURRECTION OF THE BODY**.

This is the belief that when people die they stay in the grave until the end of the world and wait for the resurrection at the **LAST DAY** or the **DAY OF JUDGEMENT**.

On this day, God will resurrect every person who has lived and they will face judgement. Those who have fully believed in Jesus and received his forgiveness for sin will be taken to heaven and those who have not taken to hell.

Christians believe this because:

- **NOT A GHOST** - Jesus' body was raised from the dead and he was seen with an identifiable body by his disciples. In **LUKE 24:39**, Jesus invites his disciples to reach out to touch him, and tells them that he is not a ghost

- **ST PAUL** - Teaches that:

  "The body that is sown is perishable [ie, it dies], and is raised imperishable. It is sown in a natural body; it is raised a spiritual body"

  1 Corinthians 15: 42-44

- **NICENE CREED** - The early creeds of Christianity state this belief: the Nicene Creed talks about, "the resurrection of the dead", whilst the **APOSTLES CREED** specifically mentions "the resurrection of the body and life everlasting."

However, the Bible finds it difficult to explain what this body will be like. As noted above, after Jesus' resurrection, he appeared to his disciples in bodily form. But on another occasion, he appeared through a locked door (**JOHN 20:19-20**). The resurrected body seems to be similar but different to the one Jesus had on earth.

DENNIS BROWN says resurrection is:

"Not about resuscitating a dead body - bodies disintegrate and turn to dust. It is about re-creating humans as spiritual individuals."

Even Paul find it difficult to explain this body - In 1 Corinthians 15:52, he says that:

"The dead will be raised imperishable, and we shall be changed. For the perishable must be clothed with the imperishable, and the mortal with immortality."

The life of Jesus, the teaching of the Bible and early Christian creeds are all important sources of authority which have shaped and influenced Christian beliefs.

Dualism

However, other Christians, mainly within the Protestant tradition, do not believe in the resurrection of the body, but the **IMMORTALITY OF THE SOUL**.

This belief in based on a position called **DUALISM**, which is the idea that the human being is made up of physical matter and an immaterial soul. After living **ONE LIFE**, the soul **LEAVES THE BODY** and the body stays in the grave and decays. Unlike the physical body, **THE SOUL DOES NOT DIE**, but continues to exist in a spiritual realm. This means that the **SOUL IS IMMORTAL**, and goes straight to heaven or hell after death. There is no need for a body in a spiritual place like Heaven.

This is based on the belief that:

- **NO WAITING UNTIL JUDGEMENT DAY** - Jesus promised the dying thief on the cross the dying thief on the cross that, after his death, he would be in Paradise with Jesus that same day (Luke 23:43). There would be no waiting around until the Day of Judgement

- **SPIRITUAL BODY** - A different interpretation of St Paul's teaching in **1 CORINTHIANS 15** which talks about a "spiritual body". Many Christians take this as meaning that there is no physical resurrection but it is the soul that survives death

Many Christians, and some within the Protestant tradition, reject this view, as it degrades the place of the body which God has created. Church of England Bishop **TOM WRIGHT** writes:

> *"I have often heard people say, 'I'm going to heaven soon, and I won't need this stupid body there, thank goodness.' That's a very damaging distortion. In the Bible we are told that you die, and enter an intermediate state. This is 'conscious', but compared to being bodily alive, it will be like being asleep. This will be followed by resurrection into new bodies."*

Wright goes on to say that:

> *"At no point do the Gospels say,*
>
> *'Jesus has been raised, therefore we are all going to heaven.'*
>
> *The Bible says that Christ is coming here, to join together the heavens and the earth in a new act of creation."*

This is closer to the Roman Catholic belief that, after death, the soul immediately faces God in what is called the **PARTICULAR JUDGEMENT**.

At that point it is decided if the soul is worthy of heaven, hell or purgatory (see Christian beliefs for explanation of purgatory)

At the end of time, at Jesus' second coming (called the **PAROUSIA**), a **GENERAL JUDGEMENT** will take place, and the body will be reunited with the soul. This new unified person will have the same qualities as the risen Christ.

This belief is based on the resurrection of Jesus and his teaching, the traditions of the RC Church and the Creeds. Further Bible teaching that is important includes **JOHN 5:28-9**, where Jesus says:

> *"For an hour is coming in which all those in their tombs shall hear his voice and come forth. Those who have done right shall rise to live, and those who have done what is evil will rise to be condemned."*

The Roman Catholic tradition therefore teaches that there is need for both body and soul to continue after death. The soul continues in existence after physical death, but the body and soul are not reunited until the final judgement of God.

> *"For this reason Christians are joyously awaiting the Second Coming of the Lord as the moment of total salvation of one's whole being - soul and body - and as the full and definitive fulfilment of their hope … this joy is expressed by Paul in the words, 'and so we will be with the Lord forever' (1 Thessalonians 4:17)"*

Christian beliefs about Heaven and Hell

‣ An outline of heaven and hell is given in the Christian beliefs section.

Many Christians believe that total belief in Jesus and the acceptance of his forgiveness is the only way to receive life after death in heaven. A person has to receive God's grace through repentance in order to know the benefits of salvation, including eternal life - see Christian belief section for more description of this.

This is based on teachings in the Bible, such as **JOHN 3:16**:

> *"For God so loved the world that he gave his only Son, that whoever believes in Him shall not perish but have eternal life."*

And Ephesians 2:3-6 and verses 8 and 9:

> *"We were, by nature, deserving of God's wrath. But because of his great love for us, God, who is rich in mercy, made us alive with Christ even when we were dead in sin. It is by grace you have been saved. And God raised us up with Christ and seated us with him in the heavenly realms in Christ Jesus. It is by grace you have been saved, through faith - and this is not from yourselves, it is the gift of God."*

Other Christians believe that God will take account of what good deeds a person has done. In

MATTHEW 25, Jesus teaches that those who have taken opportunity to help the poor, naked, homeless and other vulnerable people, have shown God's mercy, and will therefore be rewarded after death.

Other indicators of life after death

▸ The paranormal

This involves events that don't seem to have a scientific explanation, and are thought to have a supernatural cause. These can include ghosts and hauntings and even things such as communication with the dead.

Many Christians recognise that life is more than physical and the paranormal gives some insight into a spiritual reality. **EPHESIANS 6:12** says that the battle for Christians is, "not against flesh and blood, but against the powers of this dark world and against the spiritual forces of evil in the heavenly realms." However, Christianity does not support attempts to contact the dead.

▸ Remembered lives

Studies have been carried out that seem to suggest, in some cases, that people can remember events from a previous life. In a detailed study by **DR IAN STEPHENSON**, 3,000 cases of children who remembered details from a previous life were studied with the conclusion that many such memories have no easy way of explanation. However, Christians do not believe in reincarnation, so would suggest that these stories are not necessarily evidence of life after death.

▸ Logic, comfort and reward

Some Christians argue that this world very obviously does not have a sense of justice. Innocent people seem to get hurt, and those who commit crimes get away with it. **IMMANUEL KANT** said that if life is rational, there must be a place where the good are rewarded with happiness, as they do not seem to have that reward in this life. Christians believe that God ensures that justice is done through the provision of the afterlife.

CHRISTIAN RESPONSES TO ARGUMENTS AGAINST LIFE AFTER DEATH

Atheist Professor of Mathematics, **BERTRAND RUSSELL** was once asked what happens when a person dies. He replied, "you rot." **ATHEIST** and **NON-RELIGIOUS** views concerning life after death include:

The idea of life after death has been invented to give people comfort when facing the inevitable and sad fact of death

Religious beliefs which offer life after death correspond to the emotional and psychological need that humans have surrounding death and the fear of death. **FREUD** argued that people find it difficult to believe that death is the end of their own existence or that of their loved ones, and long for continued existence. Offering life after death gives comfort and hope and suggests that life (and death) has meaning.

Atheists argue that putting forward a belief to help people deal with the fact of death does not mean that that belief is true.

STEPHEN FRY recently said that:

> *"Wanting something to be true is not the same as it being true."*

Suggesting that people can live after death stops people making the most of this life and facing up to the reality of death as the end of one's existence.

Professor **RICHARD DAWKINS** suggests that we have invented the notion of a soul because we cannot face up to how brutal life is at times, and random events which result in death and suffering seem to have no purpose. It is better to accept the nature of this life and get on and deal with it, finding meaning and purpose now rather than hope there is some sort of justice after death. We should choose to do good because it is the right thing to do, and not because we hope we will get rewarded for it.

▶ **Christian responses**

- **PSYCHOLOGICAL NEED** - Some Christians argue that the psychological need for life after death must come from somewhere as it is widespread. From an evolutionary perspective other psychological needs, such as the desire to overcome loneliness, and for comfort and hope are not seen as things we should get rid of, as they help us with our survival. Atheists have to say where such a need for the afterlife comes from.

- **LIVING IS THE PRIORITY** - Though belief in life after death is important, many Christians argue that the priority is getting on with this life and living well now. Christians might argue that belief in life after death and working hard now to make the best of this life are not contradictory.

- **DEATH IS A RESPONSIBILITY** - Evangelical Christians who maintain the presence of a real hell facing people after death say that this is not really a comfort at all, but a responsibility to be faced.

Lack of evidence

Many atheists argue that there is no evidence that humans survive death. No one has returned to prove that it exists. The theories that science argues for are backed up by evidence.

Human beings are just physical - a position known as **MATERIALISM**. There is nothing immaterial about people, which means that when we die, we die, and our atoms will go on to form other things. There is no evidence to suggest we are not just physical.

There is a lack of evidence that the soul, or mind, could live independently of the body. Changes to the brain affect a person's personality, demonstrating that personality is dependent on the physical nature of a person, and a **PERSONALITY** - or indeed a person - cannot exist without a body.

▶ **Christian responses**

- **WHAT KIND OF PROOF** - It is difficult to know what evidence would count for life after death if that life after death takes place outside of earth

- **FAITH** - There are many things that we believe in life, such as that we have a purpose and that there is a meaning to life, without having the type of evidence scientists would require

- **UNEXPLAINABLE** - Science seeks to find evidence for what exists. But that is not the same as saying that everything that exists is physical. Dawkins admits that the human consciousness is a "mysterious aspect of brain activity, which neither science nor philosophy can understand", but doesn't take from this that consciousness means we have some kind of immaterial soul. However, Professor **RICHARD SWINBURNE**, a Christian, suggests that the most important aspects of our personality, such as what it is like to experience things (like the smell of beef or having a red after image when the red thing is no longer present) cannot be explained in physical terms, and supports the position that body and soul are separate.

- **JOHN POLKINGHOME** - Professor, and Priest, John Polkinghorne agrees that a soul could not live without a body, but argues that that is not what Christian tradition teaches. He argues that:

"The human soul has no natural immortality and a human life after death must include a re-embodied existence by an act of God. The Christian hope for the future is resurrection."

Further debates and disagreements about life after death

- **SUSAN BLACKMORE & SAM HARRIS** - In other debates between religious and non-religious views, the validity of near-death experiences have been questioned. Professor Susan Blackmore and neuroscientist Dr Sam Harris have said that the near death experiences used as evidence of the existence of an afterlife have actually taken place whilst some neural activity has been going on. Many Christians have responded by suggesting that these experiences are not important to faith and do not feature as important reasons why Christians believe in life after death. If there are fraudulent accounts of near death experiences or claims to have gone to heaven, these should be exposed and rejected.

- **POST CRUCIFIXION** - Many people were alive and died before Christ paid for their sins on the cross - does this mean they are in hell? Christians refer to the teaching of 1 Peter 3:18-22 which says that Jesus has offered redemption to all people through his death.

- **SOCIAL CONTROL** - Isn't the promise of life after death a matter of social control? Didn't the Church in the Middle Ages put fear into people so that they had to buy their way out of hell?

- **TREASURY OF MERIT** - The Roman Catholic tradition teaches that an indulgence is a way to reduce the amount of punishment one has to take for sins. **MORTAL SINS** cause **ETERNAL PUNISHMENT** and **VENIAL** (minor) **SINS** cause **TEMPORAL PUNISHMENT**. Good works, prayers, giving and suffering build up merit, and from the **TREASURY OF MERIT** the Church can issue an indulgence which can be applied to the temporal debt of a person, reducing the remaining consequences of sin. The Roman Catholic Church does not suggest that indulgences should be or were used for social control or to allow people to **BUY THEIR WAY INTO HEAVEN**.

EUTHANASIA

The word euthanasia means **GOOD DEATH** and is sometimes known as **MERCY KILLING**. There are different types of euthanasia:

▶ **Voluntary euthanasia**

A person's life is painlessly ended after they have requested that to happen. This could be in a situation where a person is terminally ill, and wants to avoid a painful and prolonged end to life, or in a situation such as a battlefield where a soldier has received life-threatening injuries and asks someone to end their life.

▶ **Non-voluntary Euthanasia**

A person's life is painlessly ended when they are unable to ask for it to be ended, but there is reason to believe that this is what the person would want, eg when the person is on a life support machine.

▶ **Assisted Suicide**

A person assists someone else to die by providing the means to commit suicide.

Switching off a life machine when a person has been declared as brain dead is not considered euthanasia

▶ **Active Euthanasia**

Where a doctor actively ends a life, by means of something like a lethal injection

▸ **Passive Euthanasia**

When medical treatment, including life support, which is keeping a person alive, is withdrawn. Or when treatment is not given that would help keep a person alive.

Because of the principle of the sanctity of life, many Christians are against euthanasia. However, there are mixed Christian views

Christian arguments against euthanasia

- **ALL LIFE IS SACRED** - Despite the person being in pain or incapacitated. Committing euthanasia would suggest that value should be given only to life that is active, but this goes against the principle that all life is sacred. Taking life is murder, no matter what state the person is in.

- **JOB 2:1-10** - God knew what suffering was going to come to Job, and it was allowed. Job learnt lessons about God's nature in suffering that he would not have learnt through any other way. Ending his life when in pain would not have enabled Job to understand more about God, himself and the nature of life. Life is to be valued, however hard, and it is wrong for another person to judge the value of another's life and decide to take it away.

- **GOD KNOWS SUFFERING** - Jesus himself suffered and so understands what terrible pain is like. This gives comfort for the person to endure pain and know that God is aware of what it is like to suffer.

- **GOD HAS A PLAN FOR YOU** - God has a plan for each person, and the taking of life, particularly through suicide, is not allowing that plan to take place. A person should not assist another person to commit suicide, but should help them through their pain.

- **NOT OUR DECISION** - There are some decisions that are not ours to make. God alone decides when life begins and ends. Euthanasia oversteps this line.

Alternatives to Euthanasia

▸ Hospices

As an alternative to euthanasia, Christians have been actively involved in initiating and supporting the **HOSPICE MOVEMENT**. Hospices are specialist homes which care for the terminally ill:

- **PAIN FREE** - By making life as pain free as possible, so that the end of life and death is as peaceful as possible; alongside preparing a person for their death, hospices also arrange for those who are dying to get dressed and out of bed, and have manicures etc, so that life is as "normal" as possible.

- **FACING DEATH** - By caring for people by helping them face up to death; the person dying, relatives and friends are given the chance to discuss death and dying, and offered emotional, practical, social and spiritual support.

▸ Palliative Care

Care for the terminally ill is known as **PALLIATIVE CARE**. Christian hospices include St. Christopher's, founded by **DAME CICELY SAUNDERS** in 1967. Her care for the dying was motivated by her Christian faith, though the hospice welcomes people and staff all faiths or none. Her motto was, "you matter because you are you and you matter until the last moment of your life."

The Christian Hospice movement notes that,

"We are now always able to control pain in terminal cancer in the patients sent to us…euthanasia as advocated is wrong … it should be unnecessary and is an admission of defeat."

Christian Support for Euthanasia

However, there are alternative Christian arguments that, in some cases, would support euthanasia. Generally, Christians would be against voluntary euthanasia, although in special cases of extreme distress some might allow it. Some Christians might support non-voluntary euthanasia:

- **CONSIDER QUALITY OF LIFE** - The quality of life should also be taken into consideration as well as the **SANCTITY OF LIFE**. If life that has no meaningful quality is ended painlessly, bringing relief to the person and their family, this could be the lesser of two evils. Some Christians support turning off the life support machine where there are no signs of life.

- **END OF SUFFERING** - Jesus was compassionate, and therefore would support the ending of suffering, particularly when a person is terminally ill and in pain. In the **GOLDEN RULE**, Jesus taught that people should "do to others as you would have them do to you" (**LUKE 6:31**), which could be applied to euthanasia as putting someone out of pain if that is what you would like to happen to you.

- **SUFFERING IS NOT LOVE** - Some Christians who support the approach of **SITUATION ETHICS** to moral dilemmas suggest that a loving thing can be to put a person out of pain. The opposite is true - it is not loving to see a person continue to suffer, and questionable whether any useful lessons are being learnt through such pain.

- **LIFE ENDS NATURALLY** - The Roman Catholic Church does not agree with any action that kills a patient and condemns euthanasia outright. However, it does not support the idea of extending life for a short period of time using **EXTRAORDINARY MEANS** or **OVER-ZEALOUS TREATMENT**. This allows for the withdrawal of treatment, but the act of withdrawing treatment does not end the person's life - life naturally ends

- **PALLIATIVE CARE** - In addition, the Catechism of the Catholic Church allows for the use of painkillers to relieve suffering, even if these risk shortening a person's life, as long as the intention is not to end life. Neither of these examples is euthanasia; instead, the Roman Catholic Church supports palliative care.

Atheist and Humanist Approaches to Euthanasia

Although within atheism and humanism there are different positions with regard to euthanasia, key principles which guide many atheists and humanists to support the option of a person ending their life include:

- **LIFE BELONGS TO THE PERSON, NOT TO GOD** - Therefore, the first consideration should be to respect the decision of the person and if this includes the considered wish to die without pain it should be allowed. People are **AUTONOMOUS BEINGS** - that is, in charge of their own destiny

- **PEOPLE ARE MORE IMPORTANT** - The sanctity of life principle would allow suffering to continue. The **QUALITY OF LIFE**, and a person's **DIGNITY** and **HAPPINESS**, is more important

- **SLIPPERY SLOPE** - However, others argue that there could be a **SLIPPERY SLOPE** where although the intention of the law is to allow euthanasia in specific cases, more people might take the option. An argument could then be made in the future to allow euthanasia for those who are not terminally ill, but who do not want to continue living. In this way, the original intention "broadens out" or starts to slip.

- **DOCTORS SAVE LIVES** - Others are concerned that it could change the relationship between doctors and patients. Doctors are trained to save lives, not offer to end them.

Christian Responses to the Euthanasia Debate

Christians would disagree with first two points because of the belief that life is a gift from God, but could easily support the 2 other points.

Representing the Church of England's stance against euthanasia, in September 2015, the Archbishop of Canterbury argued that:

- **ILLEGITIMATE** - It is not good for a society to legitimise suicide. Suicide is a tragedy and making this option available might replace personal compassion in favour of a clinical procedure. The UK should avoid going down this road.

- **FAMILY BURDEN** - Many elderly people might be put at risk by a change of the law; people may feel that they should take the option of euthanasia instead of being a burden on the family and this has happened in Oregon, where euthanasia has been legalised. The current law protects vulnerable people.

- **LIFE IS DEVALUED** - We could end up with a society where life is devalued, and no longer seen as worth protecting, honouring and fighting for.

THE NATURAL WORLD

Christianity teaches that humans are **STEWARDS** of God's earth. This does not mean that the earth belongs to them, but that they have been placed in a role of **CARING FOR THE ENVIRONMENT AND ALL ITS LIFE FORMS**.

This is based on teaching from the Bible, and in particular the Creation stories:

- **GENESIS 1:26** - Also then again in verse 28, God says to "man" that he has "dominion over the fish of the sea and over the birds of the heavens and over the livestock and over every creeping thing that creeps on the earth"

- **IMAGE OF GOD** - This verse is in the middle of the teaching that man and woman are made in the image of God. This gives Christians some clues about how they are to carry out their **DOMINION**. For example, with wisdom and compassion, which are two of the characteristics of God

- **PSALM 8:6-8** - The author says that God has made humanity, "rulers over the works of God's hand; he has put everything under their feet: all flocks and herds, and the animals of the wild, the birds in the sky, and the fish in the sea, all that swim the paths of the seas."

- **PSALM 24:1** - This does not mean that the earth belongs to, or is owned by, humanity, as is clear from: "The earth is the Lord's and everything in it." However, Christians believe that this teaching places on humanity the responsibility to **CARE AND PROTECT THE EARTH, AND TRY TO WORK SO THAT IT FLOURISHES**. This includes responses to threats to the natural environment including pollution, global warming and the use of natural resources,

In The Christian Declaration on Nature, in 1986, Christians declared that:

- **MAGNIFICENCE** - God created all that there is and all creatures depend on him for their existence. The creation shows something of God's beauty, love, wisdom, majesty, glory and power

- **EVERYTHING IS GOOD** - At creation, God declared that everything is good. Everything has been brought into existence by God to be dependent on each other and give glory to him. Man, made in God's image, has been trusted with a unique role of dominion to show God's goodness.

- **DO NOT DESTROY** - This does not give a licence to abuse or spoil, squander or destroy what God has made; it involves stewarding, and working in partnership with God's creatures, and God. Man should not destroy himself or God's treasures on earth. Not following his duty properly is an offence to God. The first disobedience man showed to God resulted in domination, injustice and exploitation, which has made it difficult for man to live in harmony with one another and the rest of creation.

- **GOD WILL TRANSFORM** - However, God has rescued humanity through Jesus, who will bring all creation back into its right order in the new heaven and earth. God will not destroy, but rather transform what he had made

Benedictine monks, St Francis of Assisi and other Christians throughout history have given an example of how to live in harmony with nature. Every work should lead to mutual enrichment of man and creatures, as the earth faces great challenges, such as:

- **UNCONTROLLED USE OF TECHNOLOGY** - For immediate economic growth

- **LITTLE CONSIDERATION** - Of the earth's resources and their renewal

- **THE THREAT OF WAR**

- **CONSUMER-ORIENTED SOCIETIES** - Which exploit resources, and force urban developments

- **EXCLUSIVE PREOCCUPATION** - With the present without thought for the future

Whilst declaring it is against any acts of humans, such as war, that do not enable people and the environment to flourish, The Declaration affirms support for scientific research which will benefit the environment, the priority of moral values over technological advances, and strivings for justice, truth and peaceful coexistence.

Christian responses to threats to the natural world: Pollution, global warming and the use of resources

> *"Pollution harms the unborn, casting damage that lasts a lifetime. Dirty air and water has serious consequences for the health of our children and other vulnerable populations like the elderly. This is why pro-life Christians must lead the charge on clean energy."*

Increased use of the earth's natural resources, pollution of the air, land and water, and a change to the earth's climate, have resulted in challenges to humanity and the environment:

▸ Green Christian

The organisation Green Christian encourages Christians to take action to work in more sustainable ways with God's creation. It also produces research, and has recently lobbied the Church of England to stop including gas and oil companies in its investment portfolio. In The Big Shift campaign it has encouraged government to invest in cleaner energy.

▸ Tearfund

Christian relief agency, Tearfund, has launched a new campaign, **ORDINARY HEROES**, to help give people ways of getting involved in making a difference. It is aimed at combatting climate change and global inequality and involves:

- **FOOD SHARING** - To make the world more just and sustainable

- **RENEWABLE ENERGY** - Switching energy to 100% renewable electricity

- **ENVIRONMENTAL RESPONSIBILITY** - Encouraging churches to be more environmentally responsible

▸ Roman Catholic Environmental Campaign

POPE BENEDICT XVI, as part of the Vatican's Environmental Campaign, called pollution one of the most-deadly modern sins. As well as making a commitment for The Vatican to become a carbon-neutral nation, he urged against rapidly adopting genetically modified crops and encouraged responsible lifestyles to help the poor and future generations.

In his inaugural speech, **POPE FRANCIS** said that exploiting the environment will hurt the poor. He encouraged people to be:

"Protectors of creation, protectors of God's plan inscribed in nature, protectors of one another and of the environment"

A ROCHA is a Christian conservation organisation striving to put **BIBLICAL STEWARDSHIP** principles into practice in projects, education and cooperation, working towards the sustainable use of resources in God's world.

Christians might choose to support non-religious environmental organisations such as **GREENPEACE** or the **WORLD WIDE FUND FOR NATURE**, as they would agree with the principles of such organisations.

Christian responses to Animal Rights

Many Christians believe, that, whilst it is not good to abuse animals, the order given in the creation stories suggests that **HUMANS ARE MORE IMPORTANT THAN ANIMALS**. This means that many within the Christian tradition support the use of research on animals for the development of medicines, but not for things such as shampoo or make-up. The key issues include:

- **DO ANIMALS HAVE SOULS?** - Christianity teaches that animals do not have souls. This results in the view that animals have **FEWER RIGHTS** than humans. The principle of the sanctity of life applies only to humans.

- **HOW SHOULD WE USE ANIMALS?** - Both the Roman Catholic Church and the Church of England accept the use of animals for scientific research, where the research will benefit human health and wellbeing.

- **ANIMAL RESEARCH METHODS** - Christians are concerned that animals are treated with kindness and do not undergo undue suffering

- **ANIMALS FOR FOOD** - There are no rules in Christianity which outlaw the eating of animals for food, but some Christians feel an ethical obligation to be vegetarian. Christians want the conditions in which animals are kept to be good, and for the slaughter of animals to be carried out in a humane way.

In contrast to Christian approaches, animal rights have more prominence within **UTILITARIANISM**. There are different strands and approaches within this ethical theory:

- **ANIMAL PAIN** - The pain of sentient animals should be taken into account. Such beings can feel pain and joy and their suffering must be taken into consideration when deciding what to do. In Utilitarianism, an action must increase the overall amount of happiness.

- **JEREMY BENTHAM** and **JOHN STUART MILL** - They established Utilitarianism and argued that "the status of nonhuman animals should be respected as equal to that of animals." **PETER SINGER** argues that in each situation we should equally consider the interests of animals.

- **THE GREATER GOOD** - For many utilitarianists therefore, using animals for food or research can only be acceptable if the happiness that their exploitation causes is greater than the harm it causes. The suffering caused to animals to give momentary pleasures to humans (such as eating) does not increase the total happiness in the world. Therefore, "such exploitation cannot be considered morally legitimate according to utilitarianism."

However, if performing medical research on a small number of animals maximises the overall happiness, this can be justified under utilitarianism.

NEED MORE HELP ON MATTERS OF LIFE & DEATH?

Use your phone to scan this QR code

Religion, Peace & Conflict

(1RBO/Area of Study 2)

Beliefs
See Religion & Ethics

Crime & Punishment

Living the Christian Life
See Religion & Ethics

Peace & Conflict

Crime & Punishment

KEYWORDS

- **CAPITAL PUNISHMENT** - The death penalty; punishment by execution

- **CRIME** - An action, or failure to carry out an action, that breaks the law and is punishable by law

- **DETERRENCE** - The use of punishment to deter or discourage other people from offending

- **FORGIVENESS** - To grant pardon for an offence or sin

- **JUSTICE** - The quality of being just, impartial or fair

- **PROTECTION** - Punishing a criminal in such a way that they cannot harm other people or society, eg by keeping them in prison

- **PUNISHMENT** - A penalty given to a person because they have broken the law

- **REFORMATION** - Punishment which aims to change someone's behaviour for the better

- **RESTORATION** - Restoring someone who has done wrong

- **RETRIBUTION** - Punishment which is carried out for the purposes of repayment or revenge for the wrong act committed

- **TORTURE** - The action of inflicting severe pain; in this section, inflicting pain as a punishment or to force a person to say or do something

CHRISTIAN ATTITUDES TOWARDS JUSTICE

Justice is important to Christians because:

- **GOD IS JUST** - God's nature is to be just, and Christians want to reflect His nature in the way that they live

- **ALL ARE EQUAL** - All people are equal and therefore deserve to be treated with fairness and justice

- **RIGHTEOUSNESS IS BLESSED** - The Bible teaches Christians to carry out justice; Jesus taught that people should treat all people with fairness and dignity. He taught that those who work for righteousness (doing the morally right thing) are blessed

- **JUSTICE IS REWARDING** - Those who work for justice for the most vulnerable shall be rewarded. See Matthew chapter 25

In the Old Testament, the Law (the 10 commandments and other commandments about how to live) was provided so that people could live in a way that treated people in a just manner, which reflected the justice of God. This was to protect and preserve the dignity of every person, made in the image of God.

In the Old Testament book of Micah, chapters 3 and 6, the nature of justice is outlined:

> *"Micah 3 teaches that God is against those leaders that 'judge for a bribe.' And against priests who 'preach for a price', and prophets who 'tell fortunes for money.'"*

God warns His people that disaster will come to them if they cheat and do not carry out justice.

In Micah 6 God says that he cannot stand **DISHONEST SCALES** and **FALSE WEIGHTS** and is against those that lie and are dishonest. He is not interested when people seem to do the right thing in public and make a big show of giving but are trying to get away with things that are unfair.

The summary of God's view of justice is given in Micah 6 verse 8:

> *"God has shown you, O man, what is good. And what does the Lord require of you? To act justly and to love mercy and to walk humbly with your God."*

This passage of the Bible gives Christians key instructions about the nature of justice, as it combines humble respect for God with an attitude of justice with an approach of mercy.

Christians are keen to support those who have been victims of injustice to ensure that they receive justice. Christians are taught, through the Bible, to protect the vulnerable and care for those who are likely to be treated with injustice. For example, Christian Aid has launched a campaign to work against gender injustices where women are the victims of a lack of justice and equality. Hope for Justice is a Christian charity trying to bring justice and hope to the victims of sexual trafficking.

Although not motivated by the idea of bringing God's justice on earth, or reflecting his nature, many people who take a humanist or atheist approach to issues of injustice work to help bring justice for victims. Because a central aim of Humanism is for humanity to flourish, it is important that where that is not happening, people act to restore dignity, hope and justice.

The British Humanist Association notes that:

> *"Man should show respect to man, irrespective of class, race or creed. [This is] fundamental to the humanist attitude to life. Among the fundamental moral principles, he would count those of freedom, justice, tolerance and happiness"*

Christians, atheists and humanists have the same aim of bringing about justice for victims and protecting and supporting those who are likely to face injustice. Movements such as Common Ground: Conversations among Humanists and Religious Believers outline the things about which Christians and Humanists agree; work to help support refugees fleeing persecution has seen groups with different beliefs working together to support victims of injustice.

Historically, Christians have worked with a range of organisations to bring justice for the vulnerable, including the Jubilee 200 Campaign, which resulted in the UK Government releasing the debt it was owed by some of the poorest countries of the world.

CHRISTIAN ATTITUDES TOWARDS CRIME

For Christians, there is a difference between a sin, when God's law is broken, and crime, which is the breaking of State laws. Christians believe that a good society, which respects all people, will have a fair system of law, as this will enable it to:

- **PROTECT** - The weak and vulnerable
- **ESTABLISH** - A good society where people feel safe and know what actions and behaviours are within the law
- **PROVIDE** - Fair treatment to the victim, and both fair punishment and treatment to those who have committed crime
- **CARRY OUT** - Justice for all

The causes of crime are complex and many factors contribute to why a crime takes place. These include:

- **THINGS** - Need or want for money or possessions
- **ADDICTION** - The need to feed an addiction
- **EMOTIONS** - Envy, anger or revenge

- **PRESSURE** - Family upbringing and peer pressure

- **GREED**

- **POVERTY**

- **MENTAL ILLNESS**

The nature of crime is also complex and ranges from theft and robbery, to harm to a person, damage to property, to tax evasion and fraud. Crime can be committed by people of a range of backgrounds, with deliberation or spontaneously, against strangers or those known to the person, or a group or corporation, and over differing lengths of time.

Christians work to eliminate the causes of crime as well as help those who have been affected by the crime, both the perpetrators and the victims. Christians recognise that criminals need to be deterred (put off) from committing a crime, and so might support punishments that do that, but also attempt to uncover the root causes of crime, such as poverty, lack of teaching about right and wrong and respect for the law, and addiction.

Biblical Teaching

Christians draw support from their approaches to crime from teaching in the Bible which includes:
- **JOHN 8:1-11** - A woman who had broken the Jewish Law and had been accused of adultery, was pardoned by Jesus. After saying that no one in the crowd was in a position to condemn the woman (apart from him), he told her to "go and sin no more." In doing this, Jesus acted with compassion but still did not approve of what she had been doing. This story is useful in providing guidance for Christians.

- **MARK 12:17** - Jesus says that what is due to the State and authorities should be given to them, so Christians should show respect for the rule of Law. This is repeated by Paul in Romans 13:1 and Peter in 1 Peter 2: 13-14.

- **MATTHEW 7:1** - In this teaching, Christians are told not to judge others, as God is the judge of all. Jesus also taught people to "do to others what you would have them do to you", which means that no punishment should go against what we would desire for ourselves.

Christian action to help end crime

▸ **Prison Fellowship**

The Prison Fellowship is a Christian charity supporting the work of Christian Prison Chaplains and which aims to:

"Show Christ's love to prisoners by coming alongside them and supporting them."

It does this by praying with prisoners, giving practical support to the prisoner and their family and by trying to support former prisoners when released, so that they will not commit further crime. The Prison Fellowship has over 2,000 members in England and Wales, most of whom are volunteers.

In practical terms, this will involve:

- **INCLUSIVITY** - Writing to prisoners to help them avoid the feeling of being isolated in prison. Enabling a prisoner to feel that someone is caring for them and has remembered them can help reduce re-offending.

- **TEACHING** - Teaching prisoners about the impact that their crimes have had on their victims. The **PRISON FELLOWSHIP** believes in restorative justice, which is where the prisoner is given every opportunity to learn from and take responsibility for their crime and its impact upon victims, and be reintegrated into society to make a positive contribution. Currently, 60% of adult male offenders will reoffend within 2 years. **RESTORATIVE JUSTICE** has been shown to reduce reoffending rates by up to 27%.

- **FUNDRAISING** - Raising funds to enable prisoners to give Christmas presents to their children, and to maintain good contact with the prisoner's family, which helps to reduce re-offending.

Hebrews 13:3 reminds Christians to:

"Remember those in prison as if you were their fellow-prisoners."

▸ Street Pastors

Street pastors are volunteers from churches who receive training to go out into their local neighbourhoods at night in order to care, listen and give help to people in order to make their communities safer, particularly where people are vulnerable to the effects of alcohol and drugs.

The patron of Street Pastors, which now has 11,000 trained volunteers, notes that:

"Street Pastors is about Christians rolling up their sleeves and getting involved in practically responding to the problems of crime and safety."

Street pastors typically work from 10pm to 4am in conjunction with other agencies, and attempt to show God's love in a practical way. In this way, they work to prevent crime from happening in situations where people are not always in control of their own actions.

▸ Individual Christian responses to help prevent crime

LOCKLEAZE is one of the most socially disadvantaged communities in Bristol. St James Church, led by former football hooligan, Rev. Dave Jeal, has attempted to bring change to the local community by offering a boxing club, a gardening group, groups for young people, including a local league football club, advice and support and the offer of help to families so that generational cycles of crime can be broken. Its moto is:

"Loving the hell out of Lockleaze"

CHRISTIAN TEACHINGS ABOUT GOOD, EVIL AND SUFFERING

See also Section 1:7 regarding the problem of evil and suffering, the nature of God and Christian responses.

Christianity stresses that people are responsible for their good and bad deeds. Because people have free will, they are able to make choices about their actions and are expected to live with the consequences of them. Christianity teaches that people are capable of the highest acts of kindness and good, but also devastating acts of cruelty and evil. Evil actions are the result of humanity rebelling against God, firstly at The Fall, when humanity chose to disobey God's instructions, which resulted in sin entering the world, and then in the way they make choices which go against what God wants. People may be influenced by those around them, or the work of evil forces, such as Satan, but Christian teaching stresses personal responsibility for good and bad choices and actions. Actions which go against God's nature, including acts of violence, crime and terror, as well as natural events, can cause suffering and have devastating consequences.

In **MATTHEW 25: 31-46**, Jesus taught that people are responsible for their actions, and will be rewarded or punished according to the nature of them. Jesus says that at the end of time, people will be separated into sheep and goats, according to what they have (or haven't) done, and be judged:

- **WORTHY** - The sheep will be rewarded with eternal life because they fed the hungry and gave the thirsty something to drink

- **INVITING** - They invited strangers into their homes

- **CARING** - They clothed the naked and visited those in prison

The goats are told that they face eternal punishment because they did not do any of the above even though they had the chance to.

Jesus finishes the story by saying that the nature of good is that people do not always realise that they are doing it, but in the actions of life when people are helping to stop suffering, and treating people with kindness, they are actually serving Him.

The Christian explanation for the nature of good and evil actions is very different from the responses of humanism and atheism.

Both **HUMANISM** and **ATHEISM** teach that:

- **THERE IS NO SIN** - There is no sin causing people to do wrong, as the belief in sin requires a God who is being sinned against. Humanists acknowledge that people can be "extraordinarily cruel and unjust" but do not have a **SINFUL NATURE** as Christianity teaches.

- **NO PUNISHMENT** - There is no reward or punishment in an after-life for good or bad actions, as there is no after life or Deity to carry out that judgement. People can be good without God's help, or without the hope of reward or fear of punishment for not acting rightly. This life is not a test to see where people will spend the after-life, as some Christians believe.

- **NO EVIL** - Many humanists and atheists are reluctant to use the term "evil", as it is associated with "actions against God". If using the word evil, humanism would suggest it indicates actions which are depraved or shameful.

- **RELIGION AND SUFFERING** - Some humanist and atheist approaches suggest that belonging to a religion can cause suffering; the belief that a person has to please a Deity can mean life is lived under a weight of guilt and fear of punishment. Religion is also a cause of suffering in the world when one worldview is forced on another, and religious practices cause restrictions to the rights and freedoms that people should have.

- **RESPONSIBLE** - In agreement with Christianity, atheists and humanists agree that people are entirely responsible for their actions, and should work towards relieving suffering and pain wherever they can. But natural suffering is just suffering caused by the way the world is, rather than the result of any Fall, and people should respond with compassion and care.

- **CONSCIENCE** - Christianity, atheism and humanism would agree that everyone has a conscience and some knowledge of what it means to **DO THE RIGHT THING**. They would disagree about the cause and source of that conscience.

In response to atheist and humanist approaches, Christian teaching stresses the need for an ultimate explanation about the nature of good and evil, and why people do good and bad deeds; there is a need for a God who sees all intentions behind actions, which no one else sees. Such ultimate judgement, which only God can make, means the world is a fair and just place as everyone is "judged according to what they have done" (Revelation 20:12).

In further contrast, Christians also believe that it is God, not humanity, who defines what is good, as his nature is good (Psalm 100:5).

However, although Christian teaching stresses personal responsibility for carrying out actions which result in suffering, which will be punished, it also acknowledges that why people suffer is not always that clear.

In Matthew 5:45, Jesus teaches that:

> *"God causes the sun to rise on the evil and the good, and sends rain on the righteous and the unrighteous."*

Some people live good lives, and follow the teaching of Matthew 25, but still suffer, and other people do not seem to suffer punishment for their bad deeds. Christianity therefore stresses that the reward and punishment for actions is not necessarily in this life, but after death when God judges everyone with full knowledge of their intentions and whether their actions were good or bad. Humanists and atheists could suggest that such undeserved suffering is just the way the world is with the unpredictability of human life, and people should respond to try to relieve suffering wherever it occurs. As noted above, there is no reward or punishment post-death.

CHRISTIAN ATTITUDES TOWARDS PUNISHMENT

Punishment is intended to uphold justice in society. Christianity teaches that, to help maintain an ordered society, punishment for the breaking of laws should be in place. The nature of the punishment should respect the rights of the victim, and uphold the dignity of the criminal, even when the law has been broken. The combination of justice and compassion is a reflection of the nature of God.

In the Old Testament, the nature of punishment was to bring God's justice and to restore right relationships between those who had broken the law and their victims. When the Law was broken, God combined justice with forgiveness in his judgement, offering the chance for the person to realise the wrong they had done and reform their way of life. Christianity teaches that the combination of justice and forgiveness is reflected in the death of Christ, which shows punishment for humanity's sin, and at the same time offering forgiveness for it:

- **CAUSE AND EFFECT** - The punishment of Adam and Eve resulted in Eve having pain in childbirth, Adam finding the ground hard to cultivate, and them being driven from the Garden of Eden. Their disobedience meant that they would know death and no longer be immortal, and this punishment showed God's justice. However, it was combined with God clothing them to cover their nakedness as a sign that God had not abandoned them (Genesis 3:16-24).

- **NO REVENGE** - This same combination of deserved and just punishment, and an intention for the criminal to be restored is shown in the next chapter of the Bible. God punishes Cain for killing his brother, but orders that no one should take revenge on Cain (Genesis 4: 1-16).

- **CHOOSE TO DO WRONG** - Christianity teaches that people are to be held responsible for their actions, and, because they freely chose to do wrong, their punishment is deserved. 2 Corinthians 5:21 teaches that everyone will be judged according to the good and evil they have done.

- **GOD IS JUDGE** - Christians believe, as shown in Luke 12:35-48, that God is the judge of humanity. The parable teaches God's judgement could come suddenly, and therefore people should be living in a manner that is honouring to him and to others. It notes that those who purposely ignore doing the will of God, when they know they should, thinking that God's judgement will never come, will be punished.

- **OLD TESTAMENT** - Notes that there is a lot of emphasis in the Old Testament about punishment for sin when God's Law has been broken. In the New Testament, God has taken the punishment for that sin through the death of Jesus, and offers the chance for people to receive forgiveness, which is a consistent theme of Jesus' teaching.

- **STATE PUNISHMENT** - Christians agree that the State should punish criminals to uphold justice in society, though there are different Christian views on the aims of punishment. Church teaching stresses that religious law and State law are not the same thing, and something that might be a sin, like adultery, is not a crime as it does not break any State laws. Many churches in the UK argue that the State should maintain the balance, shown above, between deserved punishment, the maintaining of an ordered society, the rights of the victim and attempts to uphold the dignity of the criminal where possible.

CHRISTIAN ATTITUDES TOWARDS THE AIMS OF PUNISHMENT

Laws aim to put justice into practice in a society. When laws are broken, punishment takes place, and different types of punishment, which have different aims; there are also divergent Christian views on these forms of punishment:

Protection

This aims to protect society from criminals who could be a danger to people, and to themselves, if allowed to stay in society. Many Christians would agree with forms of punishment which protect society from criminals to ensure that people feel safe and society is ordered. However, Christianity stresses that the criminal should always be treated with justice, and, where possible, given the chance to reform, and, if sensible, the opportunity to contribute to society. Christians acknowledge that this is not always possible, particularly where a person has either shown no desire to reform, is a persistent offender, or is mentally ill and would continue to be a danger to society if released from prison. Christian approaches are informed by Jesus' teaching, such as:

"Judge not or you will be judged"

Matthew 7:1-2

"Forgive those who sin against you."

Luke 11:4

Retribution

This aims to make criminals pay for what they have done wrong. It is carried out to deliver some sort of justice to the victim of crime if the criminal is given a fitting sentence which pays for their offence. Protection and retribution often go together. Some Christians support this form or punishment, as it fits in with the Old Testament view of an **EYE FOR AN EYE**, which is taught in Exodus 21:22-23. Other Christians say that Jesus updated or overturned this teaching when he said that:

> *"You have heard it said, 'Eye for eye, and tooth for tooth.' But I tell you, do not resist an evil person. If anyone slaps you on the right cheek, turn to them the other cheek also."*

Matthew 5:38-39

Many Christians believe that, since Jesus died to forgive all people, the criminal's offence should be taken seriously, but any return of violence or hatred is not what God wants. The stress should rather be on both attempting to forgive and trying to reform the criminal. The Church of England stresses that, whilst God is the ultimate judge and will hold people to account for their actions, when retribution:

> *"Becomes the major aim of action against offenders, it risks locking them into negativity and failure."*

Deterrence

This aims to make the punishment of such a nature that people will be put off, or deterred, from committing a crime. Many Christians are concerned that this treats a criminal as a **MEANS TO AN END** - this means that the Law courts make a sentence particularly harsh for one criminal in order to put other potential criminals off committing a crime, but this is not treating the criminal with justice.

In **DEUTERONOMY 17:13**, the judges are instructed by God to:

> *"Purge the evil from Israel."* If they do this, *"then everyone will hear of it and be afraid and no one else will dare to act in such a way."*

In Romans 13:3-4, Paul teaches that authorities only hold terror for those who do wrong and not those who do right, and that the ruler is one who is God's servant, appointed to bring punishment to the wrongdoer. This should put people off breaking the laws put in place by the State.

However, The Church of England notes that the effect of deterrence should not be overestimated as many who commit crime might feel they have nothing to lose, and, anyway, do not have a detailed knowledge of sentencing which would put them off committing the crime.

Some people, including some Christians, support capital punishment as a means to deter other people from committing serious crime - see later section.

Reformation

This aims to provide opportunities for the criminal to reflect upon their actions, and to reform, so that they can be restored or rehabilitated into society, or, if not, to at least reform in character. Whilst the Methodist Church and other Christian denominations teach that people who break the law should be punished and that society should be protected if the criminal is likely to be a danger to the vulnerable, they also stress reform and rehabilitation of the offender. The United Reform Church notes that,

> *"Even the most depraved person is capable of reform. And that it is, 'society's role to offer the possibility of reform through systems of confinement and imprisonment which the state organises."*

The Church of England recognises that,

> *"Rehabilitation has a firm Christian basis, in the duty to forgive and show mercy, and belief in the possibility of redemption through the grace of God. No one is totally defined by their sins and failures, and the image of God in all human beings relates to potentiality as well as actuality."*

Churches recognise that there is a need for an admission by the offender that they have done wrong as a part of the process of forgiveness. The Church of England teaches that,

> *"No human system can embody the fusion of justice and mercy that is found in the Gospel of Christ, but Christians must look for ways of dealing with crime that hold out hope for both offenders and victims."*

In September 2016, Catholic Cardinal Vincent Nichols urged Catholic parishes to ensure prisoners are welcomed into their communities and helped to integrate back into society, whilst insisting that they must face the consequences of their criminal acts. He suggested that, whilst being sensible to ensure the vulnerable are kept safe, former prisoners should not have to disclose criminal sentences on initial job applications. This would help them receive fair treatment when trying to find employment; finding a job helps the former prisoner show they are reformed and aids their rehabilitation into society.

Although not stressing a Christian foundation today, The Howard League for Penal Reform was set up by Christians in 1866 to campaign for punishments that allow offenders to reform.

In Galatians 6:1-10, Christians are encouraged to watch how they live, in case they are tempted to do wrong. Because everyone is vulnerable to doing wrong, they are instructed to gently restore the person who has sinned. Verse 7 says that God knows how people have lived, and everyone will "reap what they have sown." The passage ends with the teaching for Christians to "do good to all people, as they have the opportunity."

CHRISTIAN TEACHINGS ABOUT FORGIVENESS

Forgiveness is to grant pardon for an offence or sin, and to stop blaming someone for the thing they have done wrong

In the **OLD TESTAMENT**, God is described as One who, "pardons sins and forgives'" and who "doesn't stay angry with people, but shows mercy" (**MICAH 7:18)**.

In the New Testament, God shows his nature of mercy by offering forgiveness of sin to everyone, through the death of Jesus who takes the penalty for sin. All Christian Churches teach that Jesus' death gives pardon and forgiveness for sin, which people can receive. **1 JOHN 1:9** says that,

"If we confess our sins, he is faithful and just and will forgive us our sins."

And Christians teach that if God has forgiven us, then we should forgive others. The **LORD'S PRAYER**, in Matthew 6:12, says:

"Forgive us our sins, as we forgive those who have sinned against us."

Therefore the concept and practice of forgiveness is central to Christianity, because if God has forgiven and pardoned us who have done wrong to Him, we cannot refuse to forgive and pardon others who have done wrong to us.

Furthermore, Jesus taught that forgiveness is not a ONE OFF ACT, but more an attitude. When someone asked him how many times we should forgive others, Jesus replied, "seventy times seven" (**MATTHEW 18:21-22)**, meaning that we should not count how many times we forgive others, just as God does not count our individual sins. Paul taught that, "everyone sins and falls short of God's standards" (**ROMANS 3:23)**, so Christians believe that everyone needs to live with an attitude of forgiveness to each other, as God does to us.

Jesus also taught that if people do not forgive others their sins, "your Father in heaven will not forgive your sins" (Matthew 6:15). Christian teacher John Piper suggests that this verse means that if those who call themselves Christians still hold grudges against others and refuse to pardon them, then they obviously have not understood God's forgiveness for themselves.

Christians recognise that there is the need for a balance between **FORGIVENESS** and **JUSTICE** when it comes to the punishment of criminals and the treatment of victims. It is difficult for victims to forgive people who have committed terrible crimes against them. But Christianity teaches that it is impossible for criminals to be restored into community, and given opportunity to show that they are reformed, if they are never offered the possibility of forgiveness.

For this reason, Christians, such as those who work for the **PRISON FELLOWSHIP**, try to implement **RESTORATIVE JUSTICE**. This is a process where victims of crime, the offenders and the affected community engage with each other in an attempt to bring:

> *"Deep and lasting solutions by focusing on restitution, restoration, healing, and the future."*

RESTORATIVE JUSTICE is also an attempt to move away from the focus of vengeance or retribution as the main aim of justice. In **MATTHEW 5:21-26**, Jesus teaches that it is important for **RECONCILIATION** to take place between those whose relationship has broken down. He urges his listeners to make sure they have restored relationships with those they have offended, or those who have offended them before they come to the Temple to offer gifts to God.

CHRISTIAN TEACHINGS ABOUT THE TREATMENT OF CRIMINALS

Christians believe that human rights are important, and apply to all people, including criminals. They would support, and work to implement, the UN Declaration of Human Rights. This is because:

- **MATTHEW 10:29-31** - All people are made in the image of God and loved by God as individuals

- **LUKE 5:36** - Everyone deserves the right to fair treatment, and to be shown mercy, which is a reflection of God's character

- **MATTHEW 22:39** - Christians are taught to **LOVE YOUR NEIGHBOUR AS YOURSELF**, and Jesus also taught people to **LOVE THEIR ENEMIES (LUKE 5:35)**

This teaching means that the majority of Christians are against the use of torture, as it denies human rights. **DENNIS BROWN** points out that torture is mentioned several times in the Bible (see Jeremiah 20:2 and Matthew 18:34), but on every occasion, it is the religious person who is the victim of torture and not the one who inflicts it. Jesus himself was tortured before his death (Mark 15:19).

Many Christians also believe that a person should have a fair trial and be able to access a fair process of justice. **PROVERBS 31:8-9** teaches Christians to:

> *"Speak up for those who cannot speak for themselves, for the rights of all who are destitute. Speak up and judge fairly; defend the rights of the poor and needy."*

And **PROVERBS 22:22** says that we are:

> *"Not to crush the needy in court"*

The Roman Catholic Church teaches that,

> *"Each individual is truly a person. He has a nature that is endowed with intelligence and free will. As such he has rights and duties ... these rights and duties are universal and inviolate"* [must be free from being injured or harmed]

Pope John XXIII, 1963

Many Christians support the work of **AMNESTY INTERNATIONAL**, which campaigns against the use of torture, for free and fair trials, the release of prisoners of conscience and the support of those who have not received justice. Christians might support this work as a way of demonstrating their beliefs and putting God's love into action. Christian Aid has also been involved in calling for justice for justice for people imprisoned without a fair trial. Action by **CHRISTIANS AGAINST TORTURE** was formed in 1984 to work for the total abolition of torture.

However, some Christians argue that the use of torture can sometimes be justified if the use of it would result in the revealing of information that would save lives. This would be a good outcome and therefore those who support Situation Ethics might argue that overall benefit for society has resulted.

In 2009, a survey of 742 adults in America found that 18% of white evangelicals said use of torture against suspected terrorists can often be justified and 44% said it can sometimes be justified. However, these views are against the 'official' teaching of evangelical churches in the US.

CHRISTIAN ATTITUDES TOWARDS THE DEATH PENALTY

Capital punishment, or the death penalty, was permanently abolished in the UK in 1970

However, it is still legal in over 70 countries, including 37 of 50 US states. There are different Christian views towards the use of the death penalty, with arguments against centred on the idea that life is sacred, and the taking of that life belongs to God. Christian arguments that support capital punishment stress that it is allowed in the Bible for several offences.

There are mixed **SECULAR** (non-religious) views about capital punishment. These depend on what type of punishment is thought to be the most effective. If a person thinks punishment should act as a deterrent or as retribution, then capital punishment might be supported. If such punishments are regarded as vengeful, and lacking in justice, then capital punishment will not be seen as an appropriate form of punishment.

SITUATION ETHICS argues that the morality of an action depends upon the individual situation. In each situation, the person acting should look to apply the principle of **AGAPE LOVE** to those affected. This might seem, therefore, that Situation Ethics would never agree to take a life, even of a murderer, as it cannot be a loving thing to do. However, taking a life of a serial killer could contribute towards creating a better society for many people, and no one else can get killed by that person.

The **ROMAN CATHOLIC CHURCH** has argued against this approach as it is too dependent on the wisdom of man in deciding what might be the most loving thing to do. In making ethical decisions, Christians should follow the teachings of the Church and the Bible, and not make a case by case decision as situation ethics encourages.

NEED MORE HELP ON CRIME & PUNISHMENT?

Use your phone to scan this QR code

Peace and Conflict

KEYWORDS

- **HOLY WAR** - A war declared or carried out in support of a religious cause

- **JUST WAR** - A war that is thought to be morally or theologically justified because it meets very strict conditions

- **PACIFIST** - A person who believes that the use of violence and war is wrong

- **PASSIVE RESISTANCE** - Peaceful and non-violent means of opposing a government, such as strikes or refusal to follow what are regarded as unjust laws

- **WEAPONS OF MASS DESTRUCTION (WMD)** - A nuclear, biological, or chemical weapon able to cause widespread devastation and loss of life

CHRISTIAN ATTITUDES TOWARDS PEACE

One of the Bible's titles for Jesus is **THE PRINCE OF PEACE** (Isaiah 9:6), and Christians believe that they should follow him by living at peace with one another in personal relationships, as the Bible says that "as far as it depends on you, live at peace with everyone" (Romans 12:18). Even when Jesus was threatened with violence at the time of his arrest, he resisted using violence in return and said that it was unnecessary for the temple guards to come for him with swords and clubs (Luke 22:52). For this reason, and the belief that the Bible teaches a message of peace, some Christians are pacifists.

Christians also believe that when the Kingdom of God comes on earth, there will be complete peace: At that time, people will:

> *"Beat their swords into plowshares, and their spears into pruning hooks. Nation will not take up sword against nation, nor will they train for war anymore."*

Isaiah 2:4

Other Christians believe that staying true to Jesus will inevitably involve conflict with those who do not also follow his message. In Matthew 10:34-36, Jesus said:

> *"Do not assume that I have come to bring peace to the earth; I have not come to bring peace, but a sword. For I have come to turn 'a man against his father, a daughter against her mother ... A man's enemies will be the members of his own household".*

Many Christians do not take these verses as a support for violence, but as a warning from Jesus that following him will sometimes mean going against members of one's own family.

THE ROLE OF CHRISTIANS IN PEACE MAKING

Jesus taught that people who want to follow him must **LOVE THEIR NEIGHBOUR AS THEMSELVES** (Mark 12:31), which, in practical day-to-day living, means putting into action his teaching on love, peace, justice, forgiveness and reconciliation towards everyone they meet. Christians should live lives of peace and work to make peace where there is potential conflict, as the message of Jesus was one of peace. Jesus told Peter to put his sword back in its place when he was threatened, and that **THOSE WHO LIVE BY THE SWORD SHALL DIE BY THE SWORD** (Matthew 26:52); he also said that those who follow him should practice forgiving those who do wrong against them many times (Matthew 18:22).

Key teaching of Jesus is given in Matthew chapters 5-7, where he outlines his vision for how people should live. In Matthew 5:9, Jesus says:

"Blessed are the peacemakers for they will be called the sons of God"

This has inspired many Christians to actively work to bring peace into areas of conflict.

Pax Christi - **PEACE OF CHRIST** - is a Catholic organisation which has a vision of, "a world where people can live in peace, without any fear of violence in any form.' It was founded by Catholic Christians in France in 1945 to promote reconciliation with the German people after the Second World War, and tries to put the teaching of Jesus into practice and other Christian teaching such as "seek peace and pursue it" (Psalm 34:14). It works for peace, justice and reconciliation, and promotes non-violent solutions to conflicts.

CHRISTIAN ATTITUDES TO CONFLICT

Christians recognise that there are many varied reasons for why conflict arises, and teach that sometimes the original cause of the dispute is forgotten as the difference between the conflicting groups grows. It is important for Christians therefore that the root causes and nature of the conflict are established if there is going to be reconciliation.

Christian teaching is that the root cause of all conflict is sin, which means humanity struggles to live at peace due to pride and self-centredness. In the Bible, James teaches that:

"Fights and quarrels come from your desires for pleasure, which you are constantly fighting within you. You want things but you cannot have them, so you are ready to kill; you strongly desire things, but you cannot get them so you quarrel and fight"

James 4:1-2

At an international level, Christians teach that this can be seen through:

- **DOMINANCE** - A desire for one country or a group of countries to have more power over neighbouring countries

- **EXPANSION** - A desire for more land or resources

- **SUPERIORITY** - A desire for one group to overcome and even destroy another who it feels is wrong, or opposes the truth, or who it sees as inferior

- **FREEDOM** - A legitimate desire for freedom from oppression or tyranny

As Jesus taught that those who follow him should live a life of peace, many Christians seek to find non-violent ways of solving disputes, recognising that violence can often lead to more violence, and that Jesus taught that:

"Those who live by the sword shall die by the sword".

Matthew 26:52

JUST WAR THEORY

However, some Christians will use the Just War Theory as a way in which to solve conflicts, especially when alternative solutions have been tried and failed.

According to Purches-Knab **JOSEPH FLETCHER**, the originator of Situation Ethics, argued that conscience was not something that a person has but what a person does. This means that we need to carefully work out what the best way to respond to a situation is rather than wait for divine guidance through our conscience, or go by our intuition. A person who follows situation ethics would disagree with pacifists who would never go to war or resolve conflict with violence, as they would assess each situation on its merits, and might decide that the most loving long term action, which would benefit the most people, would be to go to war or resolve conflict with violence.

ATHEIST responses to religious teaching might include the argument that many wars and conflicts have been fuelled by religious teaching, such as in Northern Ireland (Catholic/Protestant), Iraq (Sunni/Shia) and terrorist actions from militants who are inspired by their religion (Nigeria/Afghanistan). **RICHARD DAWKINS** has argued that the promise of reward in the afterlife is a very dangerous motivation for killing inspired by religious teaching, and is keen to advance humanist ideals as a basis for conflict resolution.

HUMANISTS suggest that human flourishing takes place without any reference to religion or supernatural guidance and teaching, and that, through the efforts of people interested in peace, conflicts can be resolved. Humanists also argue that religion has justified violence and conflict around the world and will continue to do so because of competing claims about which religion has the truth.

Christian Responses to Just War Theory

Christians respond to these arguments in two ways:

- **RELIGIOUS JUSTIFICATION** - Religion has been used to justify war. However, the core teachings of the major world religions are about peace and love of humanity. People who use religion as a basis for war and conflict have taken their own version of that religion and twisted it, forgetting the core teachings.

- **AN END TO VIOLENCE** - Christians, and people from many religions, have often been very active in supporting peace efforts and an end to violence and conflict. Organisations such as Pax Christi and United States Institute of Peace have worked alongside secular groups to bring peace in different regions around the world.

CHRISTIAN ATTITUDES TO PACIFISM

Pacifists refuse to fight in a war or use violence to solve conflicts because Jesus taught a message of peace. This approach is based on teaching such as:

- **THOU SHALT NOT KILL** - God's commandment not to kill (Exodus 20:13)

- **TURN THE OTHER CHEEK** - Jesus' blessing of the peacemakers and not those who wage war (Matthew 5:9), and his teaching not to resist an evil person but turn the other cheek (Matthew 5:38)

- **JESUS' EXAMPLE** - Jesus' own non-violent response to violence against him (Matthew 26:52)

- **DO UNTO OTHERS** - The instruction to do to others as we would want them to do to us (Luke 6:31)

- **NON VIOLENCE** - Jesus' teaching that he gives a peace that the world cannot give (John 14:27), and that this peace cannot be established through violence.

Pacifists also argue that violence normally leads to more violence, which is then difficult to control or stop, and that innocent people suffer in warfare.

Although there are different Christian pacifist organisations, the **QUAKERS** or **SOCIETY OF FRIENDS** is the most well-known for its stance against all forms of violence and warfare. Founded in 1650 by George Fox, the Quakers declared that no outward weapons should ever be used and that non-violence is a much more powerful approach to challenging why people are violent to one another and to changing attitudes of fear and aggression. Some Quakers served in both world wars as stretcher bearers, but did not take up arms.

DR. MARTIN LUTHER KING JR. was an American Christian leader in the 1950s and 60s who taught Christians that they should not use violence even when they were being treated with violence as they struggled for equality. Although he was not a Quaker, his teaching against violence was the same. He said that,

> *"Returning violence for violence multiplies violence ... bringing about the thing that it seeks to destroy."*

He believed that;

> *"Nonviolence is the answer to the crucial political and moral questions of our time; the need for man to overcome oppression and violence without resorting to oppression and violence. Man must evolve for all human conflict a method which rejects revenge, aggression and retaliation. The foundation of such a method is love."*

However, although Martin Luther King was against violence, he supported passive resistance, as do Quakers and other Christians. Passive resistance is when non-violent methods are used to bring about change to unjust situations. King organised peace marches, boycotts of bus services to ensure black people would be given equal treatment to whites, rallies and non-violent resistance, which became known as the Civil Rights movement.

There are divergent Christian responses to pacifism and passive resistance. Some Christians argue that a pacifist response in some situations is not appropriate, and, in fact, naive. For example, in WWII, Hitler would have not been defeated by negotiation or passive resistance, and had to be fought against in order for Europe to win against Nazism. There are some times in which a just war, where special consideration is given to ensuring the rights and safety of the innocent, is appropriate and morally justified.

CHRISTIAN ATTITUDES TO THE JUST WAR THEORY

In the first 300 years of Christianity, Christians did not fight in wars, and its leaders instructed the followers of Christ to respond with non-violence. However, after Emperor Constantine adopted Christianity as the religion of the Roman Empire in the 4th Century, the Just War Theory was established to **JUSTIFY** warfare and lay down the conditions under which war should be declared and fought. This does not override the Christian intention to work for peace, but many Christians believe, including the Roman Catholic Church, that there might be times when war is necessary to secure peace.

In the 13th Century, St Thomas Aquinas, building on the ideas of St Augustine 900 years previously, developed the Just War Theory to help Christians decide if a war was right or justified.

For a war to be just it must:

- **BE LEGITIMATE** - Be declared by the legitimate ruler or authority of the state

- **HAVE A JUST CAUSE** - Such as the resistance of aggression or injustice

- **BE JUSTIFIED** - Be fought in order to establish justice and peace

- **BE A LAST RESORT** - Be declared as a last resort

- **BE PROPORTIONATE** - Be fought using proportionate methods; war must stop when the aims have been completed and there should not be the overuse of violence

- **PROTECT THE INNOCENT** - Protect innocent civilians.

Support for the Just War Theory

- **RIGHTEOUS** - Article 37 of the Church of England states that "it is lawful for Christian men, at the commandment of the magistrate, to wear weapons and serve in the wars."

- **WORTHY OF CITIZENSHIP** - Many Christians also argue that Paul's instruction in Romans 13:1-7 to, "submit to the governing authorities" who are **GOD'S SERVANTS**, means that they should be good citizens and fight for their country, if the war declared follows the principles of the Just War Theory. Many Christian men in WWII declared that they were fighting for **GOD AND COUNTRY**, and the war was entirely justified to save Europe against an attack, after all attempts to negotiate had failed.

- **LEGITIMATE DEFENCE** In 2016, Pope Francis declared that the basic aim of humanity should be to abolish all war, but that governments, "cannot be denied the right to legitimate defence once every means of peaceful settlement has been exhausted."

- **INDIVIDUAL** - Situation Ethicists might justify war, even though individual acts of violence would be against love. If the end result of war results in terrorism or an aggressive power being overcome, then that could be a loving thing. Because Situation Ethics is a relativist theory, each case of warfare would have to be considered separately, to see if violent actions were justified to bring about a **LOVING END**.

However, those against the use of the Just War Theory, including Quakers and many Christians argue that:

- **PROPORTIONATE IS UNDEFINED** - There is no way of ensuring that the conditions of the just war can be met. Innocent suffering takes place even with highly sophisticated laser guided weaponry, and it is not clear what "proportionate" means in the theatre of war.

- **STALEMATE** - Both sides of a conflict can use the conditions of the just war to support their justification of warfare.

CHRISTIAN ATTITUDES TO HOLY WAR

Holy war is not the same as the Just War Theory

A Holy War is fought by people who believe that God is on their side. An example of a Christian Holy War is the **CRUSADES** from 1095 to around the 14th Century, which were authorised by successive Popes against the Turks to take back the holy places of Palestine from Muslim control. After the 30 years' war between Catholics and Protestants (Central Europe, 1618-1648), it is estimated that over 2 million people died. In the English civil War of 1642-49, both sides, the Royalists and the Parliamentarians, thought their cause was supported by God.

In the **OLD TESTAMENT**, there are several passages which seem to support either the defence of God's people against an invader (against the Amalekites in Exodus 17:8-16) or the attack to conquer land. In Joshua 6, the Israelites are given specific instructions by God to capture the land that they believed was promised to their ancestor Abraham. God seems to authorise the war, and enable the Israelites to win without using conventional weapons which makes this a classical example of a Holy War. All the inhabitants of the city are killed and the city itself is burned, and this is held as a great and justified victory in the history of the Israelites.

Although Holy War is not established as a tradition in the **NEW TESTAMENT**, the fact that the Crusades took place at the height of the Church's power in Europe in the Middle Ages, suggests that Christian leaders at that time thought that a Holy War was justified. However, many Christians do not still have that view, and recently Christians have walked the route of the Crusades as a pilgrimage of forgiveness and reconciliation. Many Christians in the UK though were disappointed when President George W Bush said that the war in Iraq was a **CRUSADE**, as such language is still **HARMFUL TO PEACE**.

Although in Matthew 10:34-40, Jesus says that he has come to bring a sword and not peace and that he will divide families, this is not normally interpreted as a call to war. Jesus' teaching that those who follow him must be prepared to give up their life for him, indicates the degree to which following Jesus must be a priority over any relationships.

ATHEIST and **HUMANIST** attitudes to Holy War would be to condemn it as both unjustified and misguided. They would point to the countless lives lost in holy wars as evidence of the danger and destruction that supposed Divine authority and justification for war can lead to. Following the attack on the **TWIN TOWERS** in 2001 by people who claimed to have religious justification for carrying out the killing of over 3,000 people, Richard Dawkins suggested that religious ideas such as that were **THE ROOT OF ALL EVIL**.

Christians would respond by suggesting that the role model for them is Jesus who teaches about a kingdom of love, and that Old Testament warfare and battles such as the Crusades are not the models that Christians follow in their attitudes towards others. Whilst being a religion that supports peace, many Churches and Christians agree with the Just War Theory if every possible means of negotiation and peace-making has been tried, and there is a direct threat to the country's safety.

CHRISTIAN ATTITUDES TO WEAPONS OF MASS DESTRUCTION

There are different arguments for and against weapons of mass destruction, and particularly nuclear weapons:

Arguments for WMD

- **DEADLOCK** - If different countries have nuclear weapons, then no one country will use them, knowing that another country will be able to use their own in return

- **DETERRENT** - This acts as both a deterrent and keeps countries free from war, and so, ultimately, nuclear weapons support peace.

Arguments against WMD

- **RISKY** - Nuclear weapons are a risk to humanity and their use could signal suffering and death on an unprecedented scale

- **SLIPPERY SLOPE** - Unstable governments and leaders could get hold of nuclear weapons if they are available, and hence it is better not to have them at all.

Christian churches would use the teaching of the Just War Theory to support their opposition to nuclear warfare:

- **AGAINST JUSTIFICATION** - Innocent civilians cannot be protected in the case of nuclear war, which goes against a key principle of the Just War theory.

- **NON PROPORTIONATE** - The use of nuclear warfare can never be a proportionate use of weaponry, as they are, by their nature, made for mass destruction. Again, this goes against a key principle of the Just War theory.

The Catholic Church has stated that it should be the aim of the international community to work towards progressive disarmament. Pope Benedict XVI said in 2006 that:

> *"In a nuclear war there would be no victors, only victims. The truth of peace requires that all governments [holding nuclear weapons] agree to change their course by clear and firm decision and strive for a progressive and concerted nuclear disarmament. The resources which would be saved could then be employed in projects of development capable of benefiting all their people, especially the poor."*

Catholic organisation **PAX CHRISTI** is specifically campaigning against the renewal of the UK's nuclear submarine, Trident, and Archbishop Desmond Tutu has declared that it is time for the world's people to end the nuclear era with a celebration rather than a bang. All major denominations in the UK support multi-lateral disarmament of nuclear weapons.

In Deuteronomy 20, instructions are given by God to the Israelites to completely eradicate "anything that breathes". This is something like the equivalent to the use of a weapon of mass destruction on an area.

- **PEACE OFFERING** - Some Christians justify these verses by saying that verse 10 offers the armies who are against the Israelites the possibility of peace

- **LACK OF REFORM** - Others suggest that the enemies of the Israelites were committing detestable practices and had the chance to reform but didn't

- **LACK OF CONTEXT** - Other Christians suggest that an Old Testament practice does not justify nuclear warfare as many Old Testament practices are not continued today. Jesus has shown Christians the way to live today.

HUMANIST and **ATHEIST** responses to the teaching of Deuteronomy suggest that it is very dangerous and indefensible to have teaching in a holy book that supports the destruction of entire cities and their inhabitants. Most humanists would be against the proliferation of weapons of mass destruction as the enormous amounts of money that are spent on them could be used to benefit humanity. For non-religious reasons, atheists and humanists value life as something unique and precious, but may occasionally, as was the case in WWII, suggest that war might be the lesser evil.

In the ethical theory **UTILITARIANISM**, an action is justified if the net amount of happiness it produces outweighs the net amount of suffering it brings. This happiness can be long term, which would mean that short term pain could be outweighed by the long term net increase in human wellbeing. If countries keep a stockpile of nuclear weapons, which is what has happened since WWII, individual countries are less likely to use them, and a utiliarianist could argue that keeping them decreases the chance of war and, overall, by doing that, increases the balance of happiness

However, a utilitarianist would need to consider if the money saved through disarmament could be used to help people have better health and social care, which would increase the happiness and reduce the pain of a country's population.

Christians might respond to such an approach by suggesting that the use of nuclear weapons to keep an uneasy truce is not the best way of keeping peace. Without nuclear weapons, countries would not have the potential to completely wipe out millions of people, and less chance of accidental catastrophe. They might also suggest that adding up pleasure vs. pain, which Utilitarianism does, fails to treat each person as unique and made in the image of God.

CHRISTIAN ATTITUDES TO ISSUES SURROUNDING CONFLICT

In Luke 6:27-31, Jesus tells his followers to love their enemies and bless those who curse them. He instructs people to not hit back, but offer the other cheek to be hit, and to react with kindness to those who ask of things. He summarises his teaching by saying:

"Do to others as you would have them do to you."

In Romans 12:9 Paul directs followers of Jesus to not take revenge, and, later, to:

"Overcome evil with good"

Romans 12:20-21

Christians also believe that Jesus knows what it is like to suffer violence, and was himself a refugee who had to be taken to safety from a ruler who terrorised his people (Matthew 2:13).

These passages inform Christian responses to issues of violence, war and terror. Christians respond in such a way as they are attempting to bring "peace on earth and goodwill to all people" (Luke 2:14).

In practical ways, this means:

- **LOBBYING** - Christian organisations, such as Christian Aid, asking the government in countries such as Colombia to protect communities facing armed conflict.

- **HUMANITARIAN AID** - Calling upon Israel to lift its blockade in Gaza to allow humanitarian aid and personnel through; and putting pressure on all parties involved in the conflict to find sustainable and just resolutions.

- **PRAYER** - Praying for and supporting those affected by the pain of conflict, war and terror; Christian teaching is to "weep with those who weep, and mourn with those who mourn" (Romans 12:15) and they would attempt to do this whilst continuing to love their enemies.

In response the **BRITISH HUMANIST SOCIETY** do not believe that it is practical or particularly helpful to teach people to "turn the other cheek" as this might encourage evil actions. However, humanists and atheists would agree with Christians that revenge can bring more wrongs to a situation and would work to minimise the suffering caused by war and terror, and prevent such happening in the first place by promoting negotiation and peaceful coexistence.

Atheists and humanists would entirely reject the idea that a Deity will bring an ultimate end to all war and violence, arguing that it is up to humans to sort out issues surrounding conflict, possibly through organisations such as the United Nations. They might also argue that liberal democracies have a better record for not starting wars, and that, in fact, religion can be a source of terror, conflict and violence. In response, Christians would argue that if everyone followed Jesus' teaching to love their enemies, there would be no enemies, terror, war or conflict in the world.

NEED MORE HELP ON PEACE & CONFLICT?

Use your phone to scan this QR code

Religion, Philosophy & Social Justice

(1RBO/Area of Study 3)

Beliefs
See Religion & Ethics

Philosophy of Religion

Living the Christian Life
See Religion & Ethics

Equality

Philosophy of Religion

KEYWORDS

- **COSMOLOGICAL ARGUMENT** - The argument that God is the cause of the universe

- **DESIGN ARGUMENT** - The argument that suggests God is the designer of the universe

- **MIRACLE** - An extraordinary event which seems to break a law of science, and which is attributed to God

- **PRAYER** - An attempt to contact or communicate with God, usually using words

- **RELIGIOUS EXPERIENCE** - An occasion where a person feels they have experienced a spiritual reality, such as God speaking to them or some other supernatural event

- **RELIGIOUS UPBRINGING** - A child being raised in a way which encourages belief in God

- **REVELATION** - a divine or supernatural disclosure to humans of something about the nature of God and/or his purposes

- **VISION** - a mystical or religious experience of 'seeing' something, such as a supernatural event or spiritual figure, possibly in a dream

REVELATION AS PROOF OF THE EXISTENCE OF GOD

Revelation is very important within Christianity as it shows who God is, and proves to believers that he exists. Without it, Christians would not know the nature of God or his plans and purposes for humanity. Christians believe that God has revealed his nature and purpose for humanity through the Bible, both in the Old Testament and through the life, death and resurrection of Jesus in the New Testament.

Revelation in the Old Testament

God's **COVENANT** with Noah is outlined in Genesis. A covenant is an agreement between two parties, and in the story of Noah, God agrees to save Noah and his family from the flood which will wipe out the rest of humanity.

What Christians believe this story reveals about the nature of God and purposes for humanity:

- **EMPATHY** - God is able to see what humanity does (Genesis 6:5) and is able to feel pain at things such as evil and corruption (Gen. 6:6)

- **ACTING** - God acts in the world (Gen. 6:7)

- **WAY YOU LIVE** - It is possible for humans to please God with the way they live, as Noah did (Gen. 6:8)

- **GOD KNOWS THE FUTURE** - God knows the future and is in control of natural events (Gen. 7:4)

- **GOD KEEPS HIS WORD** - God keeps his side of the covenant (Gen. 8:1; 9:15)

- **BE FRUITFUL** - God wants his creation to be fruitful and to flourish (Gen. 9:1, 7)

God's covenant with Abraham is then revealed in Genesis 12 onwards. What Christians believe this story reveals about the nature of God and purposes for humanity:

- God has plans to bless humanity through Abraham. The revelation was that God would make Abraham the father of a great nation, the Jewish people. From the Jewish people, Jesus would be born, and this would bless 'all peoples on earth' (Genesis 12:3).

- God acts in the world (Gen. 15:5) and can change things that seem impossible, a woman in old age getting pregnant (Gen. 17:17,19). This reveals that God is not limited by human conditions.

- God keeps his side of the covenant (Gen. 17:2; 21:2).

- God wants his creation to be fruitful and to flourish (Gen. 17:6)

Whilst there are different interpretations of these stories, Christians believe that revelation of God in the Bible is proof of his existence. The revelations to Abraham and Noah are important because of what they reveal about the nature of God.

Revelation in the New Testament through Jesus

In Hebrews 1:1-4, the writer says that God has revealed himself to many people over many years, but most fully in Jesus. Through the Incarnation, Christians believe that Jesus is the full revelation of God in human form. In Hebrews it reveals him as:

- The fulfilment of all previous revelations of God in the Old Testament (vs.1 & 2)
- The exact representation of God as his Son (v.3)
- The person who has provided forgiveness for sins (v.3)
- Someone who is superior to angels (v.4)

The foundation of the Christian faith is that God has revealed who he is and his nature through Jesus, who became a man and lived, died and was resurrected. This revelation that God came to earth in Jesus is central to every other belief in Christianity. The Bible reveals that God revealed his love for the world in Jesus, who died to provide forgiveness for all humanity (John 3:16).

Philippians 2:6-11 then outlines what Christians believe about the nature of Jesus as God in human form. Christians also believe that God will reveal himself again fully at the end of the world (Revelation 22:12). These revelations prove to Christians not only that God exists, but that he is interested in the world he loves, wants a relationship with humanity, and has a plan for people. Many Christians believe that God continues to reveal who he is today, and does so when people read the Bible and come to a fresh understanding of his nature, and when they encounter God through a religious experience.

Catholic teaching stresses that the Church is the guardian of God's revelation and continues to be the vehicle through which God reveals his nature and will.

VISIONS AS PROOF OF THE EXISTENCE OF GOD

Christians believe that, from time to time, God reveals his character and plans through visions

Visions can be privately revealed in a dream, or sometimes given to people in a public setting; images such as the Virgin Mary, or Jesus, an Angel or a saint can appear vividly in a person's imagination, or the person having the vision can feel they have physically seen something. Visions can also reveal something the person hadn't realised before about God's nature, and God's plans and purposes, for them individually, and/or for others.

In **GENESIS 15,** the Bible records God giving his word to Abram (who went on to be called Abraham) in a vision. It reveals:

- God's nature of care - he tells Abram not to be afraid as God will be his shield and reward

- That Abram can communicate with God, as, in this vision, Abram and God have a conversation

- That God knows that the people who Abram will lead will suffer but that God will bless them and reward them with land

In **MATTHEW 17:1-13**, Peter, James and John are in the presence of Jesus when they see a vision of him transformed, and his face shining like the sun. They then hear a voice saying about Jesus, "this is my Son, whom I love." Although the disciples are initially terrified this vision gives them a clear idea who Jesus is, and that he is the one who the Old Testament prophets were looking forward to. This vision strengthens their faith.

Such visions can give real strength to a person's faith, can help them to understand the nature of God in a clearer way, and can help them to know God's plan and purpose for them.

OUTSIDE OF THE BIBLE, a famous story of a vision is that of Saint Marie-Bernade Soubirous, who saw the Virgin Mary at a grotto in Lourdes in southern France in 1858, and then on another 17 further occasions. Although Bernadette was not sure who the lady was who appeared to her, she revealed her identity on March 25th by saying that she was the Immaculate Conception. Over the series of visions, Bernadette received instructions to dig into the ground for water and to build a chapel on the site. Gradually, more and more people came to the grotto, and now it is a place of pilgrimage where over 100,000 people go for prayer and healing every year.

Non-religious responses to visions are that they are probably hallucinations or just part of someone's active imagination that has been misunderstood by the person. It is very difficult to provide proof for a vision, and a vision therefore does not provide a proof for God. The visions of Bernadette have received alternative explanations such as that they were **WISH-FULFILMENT** ideas of a girl who lived in extreme poverty, or that she had a series of epileptic fits which gave her the impression of bright lights.

Christians would respond by testing any vision to see if it is in agreement with the teaching of the Bible, if the person is of sound mind and if what is revealed is supported by what the Church already teaches about the nature and plans of God. Christians would also argue that as God loves humanity, it is no surprise that he communicates with people through visions and dreams. The power of a vision is also shown through the change it has made to a person's life.

Some Christians argue that God no longer gives visions as they were only for Bible times, and the Bible alone is the only way God now speaks. Others believe that they still happen but, for example, within the Catholic Church, a vision has to be accepted and recognised by the church before it can be believed as genuine. Other churches, such as those from the charismatic churches, believe God speaks through visions and should be expected to reveal himself in this way.

MIRACLES AS PROOF OF THE EXISTENCE OF GOD

Many Christians believe that, on occasion, God performs miracles on earth

Within Christianity it is understood that these extraordinary events, which break known laws of science, are not explainable in any way other than God did them. There are many miracle stories in the Bible, which Christians believe reveal something of God's power and love, and these strengthen the faith of the person who receives the miracle and those who witness it.

Although Jesus taught that people should not believe him just because he performed a miracle, people who have seen a miracle sometimes **CONVERT** to believing in God as they believe the miracle provides proof for his existence, especially where there is no scientific explanation of the event.

In **JOHN 4:43-54**, Jesus heals the son of a royal official who was close to death. The official asks Jesus to go to see his son, but Jesus pronounces that his son is better without going to visit him. The father returns to his son and finds out that he got better at the precise time when Jesus pronounced that he was well.

Because of this story and others in the Bible, Christians believe that:

- **GOD IS OMNIPOTENT** - Therefore so not limited by natural laws; he can therefore make things happen (like raising someone from the dead (**JOHN 11:1-44**), or making a blind person see (**MARK 8:22-25**), which would be impossible for people to do.

- **MIRACLES ARE A GLIMPSE INTO THE FUTURE -** Where, in **GOD'S KINGDOM**, all will be well and there will be no more sickness and death; they are a taste of that future breaking into the pain and suffering of now.

- **MIRACLES SHOW GOD'S CARE AND LOVE** - They still happen today revealing a God who is both powerful enough to perform a miracle and interested enough to respond to a specific situation.

Non-religious responses suggest that:

- **MANY OF JESUS' MIRACLES CAN NOW BE EXPLAINED** - We have a greater understanding of science and medicine.

- **THERE WAS AN ORIGINAL MISDIAGNOSIS OF A CONDITION** - When a person appeared to get better and receive a miracle, they did not have that condition or illness in the first place; or they got better at the same time at which they were prayed for as **COINCIDENCES** can and do happen.

- **PROOF OF GOD REQUIRED** - Even if an unexplained event happens, it does not provide a proof for God. It could be that the scientific explanation has not yet been found, and medicine will one day explain the healing. In fact, if God heals some people and not others, this raises questions about the character of God and whether he loves all people equally.

Although many Christians work within the medical and scientific fields, and could agree that there are things that can now be explained as scientific knowledge has advanced, there are still events that seem to be beyond anything possible, such a people raising from the dead.

Christians also argue that if God does care and love humanity, he would want to intervene, and there are many examples of people believing God has done so in history. Christians may question if every one of those events can be a coincidence or explained in other ways, though why God acts in some situations and not in others is not clear, and possibly part of a bigger plan which humans cannot see.

Miracles can still be proofs of the existence of God, though some churches believe that the miracle stories are special and powerful stories, but not necessarily literally true. They might argue that meaning can still be found in the story without the event having taken place as recorded, but other Christians argue that it is necessary and possible to believe that Jesus did the actual events as written.

CHRISTIAN ATTITUDES TOWARDS RELIGIOUS EXPERIENCES

There are different types of religious experience, both of which Christians believe can reveal that God exists, and give insight into his nature:

Private or individual religious experiences (including)

- **VISIONS AND DREAMS** - Where God is believed to have spoken to a person

- **PRAYING IN TONGUES -** A language given to believers in prayer on occasions

- **NUMINOUS EXPERIENCES** - Where a person becomes aware of a presence greater than themselves, which can inspire **AWE** and **WONDER**

- **ANSWERED PRAYERS**

- **CONVERSION** - Where a person changes their beliefs and lifestyle - in this case from non-belief to belief in God

- **MIRACLES**

Public or shared religious experiences, which include:

- **SHARED EXPERIENCES** - Where a group of believers experience the presence of God, or pray in tongues together

- **PROPHECY** - A message from God given to a person for sharing publicly, called a word of prophecy, or wisdom, or knowledge

- **MULTIPLE WITNESSES** - A miracle that is witnessed by many people

- **MANY CONVERSIONS** - All happening at the same time

Many Christians believe that religious experiences, whether private or public, are proofs for God, as they:

- **REVEAL EXISTENCE** - That he exists, as the experiences are often convincing for the person or people who have them

- **REVEAL NATURE** - Something of his nature, as the experiences are normally uplifting and life changing, and demonstrations of his love for people

An example of a religious experience is when Moses talked to God in **EXODUS CHAPTER 3**. In this experience, Moses:

- **DISCOVERED MORE** - About God's holy character - Moses had to remove his sandals in God's presence as the presence of God made the place holy

- **CERTAIN KNOWLEDGE** - Moses knew that God was the God of his ancestors, and above description, which filled Moses with awe

- **RECEIVED INSTRUCTION** - About God's plan for him and the Israelites

Professor **RICHARD SWINBURNE** argues that a religious experience might act as a philosophical argument for the existence of God as the world is normally like we experience it, which gives us good ground to believe the experience is credible. If the person giving the account can be trusted, and we would normally believe what they say, then there has to be a good argument against the account to say that it was not a religious experience.

In response, ATHEIST ARGUMENTS include:

- **WISH FULFILMENT** - The idea that the human mind is very easily persuaded to believe, and sometimes people want to believe God has spoken to them and so convince themselves that he has. This can be particularly the case when a shared religious experience is reported as people can be carried along by others. It could be that religious experiences are **WISH FULFILMENTS** as **FREUD** argued.

  Even if an experience has taken place that cannot be explained, this does not mean it is a proof for God

- **DAVID HUME** - The impossibility of the laws of nature being broken, which would question the whole of scientific understanding; David Hume said it is more likely that the law of nature has held than it has been broken in a miracle, and some other explanation is needed.

- **ALTERED MENTAL STATE** - The idea that rather than a religious experience a person is in an altered mental state through hallucinations, drugs, or other mental conditions.

None of the atheist responses would be convincing to Christians, who would suggest that

- **UNEXPECTED** - The religious experiences people have long and life changing effects; they are **NOT ALWAYS LOOKED FOR** like a wish would be, but happen to the person when not expecting them.

- **GOD CAN BREAK THE LAWS OF NATURE** - As he is omnipotent and created the laws of science.

- **MENTAL STATE** - Christians would dismiss experiences that have happened under the influence of drugs, and would question the person about their mental state

CHRISTIAN TEACHING ABOUT PRAYERS

Private and public prayers play an important role in the life of a Christian, and in the practice of the Christian Church.

The Bible encourages Christians to pray about anything, and at all times. The nature of prayer is that it is not just about asking God for things, but, rather, communication which helps to establish a relationship with God. It is important because prayer helps to sustain and encourage a Christian, and, answered prayer can strengthen and renew their faith.

- **1 JOHN 5:14-15** - Christians are told that God hears prayers, and if they "ask anything according to his will, he hears us", and answers those prayers. The key section in this verse is that Christians try to pray according to his will, as prayers which are for selfish purposes or against what God wants will not be answered.

- **PHILIPPIANS 4:6** - Encourages Christians not to be anxious about anything but to come to God with gratitude, to pray, and to present their requests to God.

- **1 THESSALONIANS 5:17** - Teaches Christians to 'pray continually' which means that communication with God should be a regular thing and a core part of Christian living.

- **MATTHEW 6:9-11** - Jesus teaches his disciples how to pray and gives them the Lord's Prayer, which Christians still say today.

Answered prayers might lead to belief in God. Many people pray who do not necessarily have a belief in God. However, answered prayer, especially if that person has told no one else about the thing they are praying for, can lead someone to put their trust in God and **CONVERT**.

THE DESIGN ARGUMENT FOR THE EXISTENCE OF GOD

The design argument states that the complex design, order and purpose seen within the universe requires a Designer, and that Designer is God

In the 13th Century, **THOMAS ACQUINAS** argued that things seem to have an order and purpose, which those things cannot have given to themselves. Things such as plants seem to have a purpose and must have been given this by someone, who Aquinas claims is God.

In the 18th Century, **WILLIAM PALEY** argued further that, if a watch, which has complex parts which work to a purpose and follow an order, needs a watchmaker, then a universe, which has complex parts on a much bigger scale and seems to work to an order and has purpose, needs a very intelligent Designer, which he claimed is God. Paley put forward other examples of complex mechanisms that have an order and purpose, such as the human eye, and which would suggest design.

The argument that Aquinas and Paley put forward is the Design argument, and Christians believe that it is a philosophical proof for the existence of God

Both scholars suggest that it is **MORE CREDIBLE** to believe that someone has put all the millions of complex features of the universe together in working order that they came together by chance or accident and somehow became ordered and purposeful.

The idea that all things work together reveals God to be both **OMNIPOTENT** and **INTELLIGENT**. And this design is evident to all people in the world. Paul writes that,

> *"Since the creation of the world God's invisible qualities - his eternal power and divine nature - have been clearly seen, being understood from what has been made, so that people are without excuse.*

Romans 1:20

The Psalms also suggest that God's wonder and majesty is revealed through his creation. In **Psalm 104**, God is praised for "making springs pour water into the ravines … making grass grow for cattle" and "plants for man to cultivate."

There are different Christian responses to whether the Design Argument is enough proof to suggest that God exists. Some Christians believe the design in the universe, as seen in the verse above, indicates that the evidence for God is obvious and people need only look around and see that the ordered and complex world shows the design of God. This is called **GENERAL** or **NATURAL REVELATION**, and some Christians believe it provides enough evidence for a person to come to a belief in God.

Other Christians argue that the world by itself does not provide enough evidence for a person necessarily to understand that God designed it, and that more revelation is needed in addition to natural revelation, such as through the Bible and Jesus. This is called **SPECIAL REVELATION**.

Non-religious responses

- **NO DEMONSTRATION** - The world does not necessarily demonstrate the design of an intelligent or omnipotent God. Suffering caused by natural disasters would not be included in the work of an intelligent designer who could have designed the world in any way he chose. Christians respond that suffering takes place in the world because of the Fall of humanity and the entrance of disorder into God's perfect design.

- **NO PURPOSE** - The world does not necessarily have design or purpose. Evolution is not designed, but simply the survival of the creature that most fits its surroundings, in a process called natural selection. Humans interpret evolution as appearing to be designed and ordered but adaptation of species is actually caused by random mutation of DNA. Some Christians respond by arguing that the whole evolutionary process is part of God's design and plan.

- **UNSUITABLE** - Analogies which suggest that just as a watch needs a watchmaker a world needs a world maker are totally unsuitable, as the world is unique and there is nothing else to which it compares. A watch with complex parts could be compared to something like another watch, or a car to look for evidence of design in both, but the world is of an entirely different nature. For this reason 18th Century philosopher David Hume rejected any argument from comparison or analogy. Christians would respond that the uniqueness of something does not mean we cannot have an idea of how it works or whether it shows similar characteristics of design to another ordered thing, such as a watch.

THE COSMOLOGICAL ARGUMENT FOR THE EXISTENCE OF GOD

The cosmological argument states that as everything that exists needs a cause, the universe also needs a cause, and that cause is God

THOMAS AQUINAS argued that everything is caused by something else. Nothing is able to bring itself into existence, but needs a prior cause. If everything needs a cause, then this chain of causes goes back and back and back. Aquinas argued that we cannot go back and back indefinitely, as there must be something that started the whole chain of cause and effect. This something must not need a cause, and must be the first cause, which he argued is God.

Aquinas put forward three ways of demonstrating God's existence from the idea of cause:

▸ God is the Unmoved Mover

- **IN MOTION** - Things in the world are in motion, that is, they **CHANGE** from one thing to another. For example, a piece of wood is changed from wood to ash when burned

- **NOTHING IS ABLE TO CHANGE BY ITSELF** - It is moved or changed by something else, for example, it is fire that changes the wood into ash

- **DETONATOR** - This chain of movers needs something to set the whole chain in motion

- **UNMOVED MOVER** - This first mover must be unmoved, otherwise the chain would keep going back and back and back and nothing would begin to move or change.

- **THIS UNMOVED MOVER IS GOD**

▸ God is the Uncaused Cause

- **SIMILAR** - This is very similar to the unmoved mover argument. All things have a cause, and nothing can cause itself

- **UNCAUSED CAUSE** - The chain of causes needs a first cause who is not caused, otherwise the chain would keep going back and back and back and nothing would be caused to exist.

- **THIS UNCAUSED CAUSE IS GOD**

▸ God is the Necessary Being

- **CONTINGENT** - Everything in the world comes in and goes out of existence, eg, humans, trees, plants etc. This is known as being contingent.

- **WILL NOT EXIST** - Because everything has the possibility of not existing, then at some point in time, that thing won't exist. For example, there will be a time when a particular person or tree does not exist

- **IMPOSSIBLE TO EXIST** - It is impossible for these things to always exist as they are contingent

- **NOTHING EXISTED** - Therefore, there was a time when no things existed if everything is contingent.

- **AT THAT TIME** - There would be nothing to bring things into existence and nothing would exist now

- **THIS IS ABSURD** - As things do exist now, so something must exist which cannot go out of existence and is what is called a **NECESSARY BEING**.

- **GOD IS THAT NECESSARY BEING** - Without him nothing would be in existence.

From the arguments put forward for God by Aquinas, Christians believe that God is **OMNIPOTENT**, and able to cause things to come into being. Unlike all other things in the universe he does not depend on anything else for his existence. He is **ETERNAL**, **NECESSARY** and **NOT CAUSED** by anything else.

Some Christians suggest that this means that God is the being who started the universe, but has nothing else to do with it now. However, mainstream Christian belief suggests that this is not the case, as God is still interested in the world today, and, if the causation and design arguments are combined with the arguments from religious experience, then there is sufficient proof for a God who is concerned for the world and humanity.

Non-religious arguments against the Cosmological argument

- **OUTSIDE AGENTS** - The suggestion that we have no idea about any outside agent existing which brings into being the entire causal chain. That complicates the matter and there might not be any need for an entire explanation - the world according to Professor **BERTRAND RUSSELL**, an atheist, **JUST IS**.

- **UNCAUSED UNIVERSE** - Even if everything within the universe requires a cause, this does not mean that the universe itself is caused. Russell said that everyone in the world has a mother, but this does not mean that the entire human race has one.

- **THE BEGINNING** - The idea that the Big Bang is the beginning of space and time; there is **NOTHING BEFORE** it as there was **NO BEFORE** the Big Bang.

- **ETERNAL UNIVERSE** - The universe could be the thing that does not need a cause, and some scientists believe that the universe itself is eternal, not God.

CHRISTIANS RESPOND by restating Aquinas' 3 arguments that without an Unmoved Mover to set the chain of motion going, and without an Uncaused Cause and without a Necessary Being, nothing else could come into existence. A first cause is a logical explanation for the existence of the universe, and fits the pattern of cause and effect which is in evidence in the world.

RELIGIOUS UPBRINGING

The Bible instructs Christians to, "train a child up in the way he should go", because "when he is old he will not turn from it", and the Church teaches that the home is the place where Christian values and beliefs should be expressed.

Christian upbringing will involve:

- **INITIATION** into the Church, such as **BAPTISM** or **CHRISTENING**, where the child is welcomed into the Church and promises are said by parents and grandparents concerning how they will raise the child up to belong to God

- **PRAYERS** - And readings from the Bible in the home environment, which encourage personal faith

- **ATTENDANCE AT CHURCH** - Including participation in worship and involvement in the church community, where Christians act as role models and continue to pass on the teaching of Christianity

- **A CHOICE OF SCHOOL** - Which respects and maybe also teaches Christian values

- **CONFIRMATION** - A further ceremony such as a confirmation service where the child is old enough to make the promises made at their baptism for themselves

All of the above ways of bringing up a child will encourage the child, and maybe lead them, to believe in God. If the beliefs of the parents and friends of the family have been spoken about in the home, and the practices of the Christian church have been familiar, then the child has a good chance of believing what has been seen and heard, and believe in God.

If the child has been taught how to pray and worship, and enjoyed being part of the Christian community, then they may continue to practice the faith and belong to the community; they may also have seen prayers answered and had a religious experience, which would lead to or support belief in God.

ATHEIST PROFESSOR RICHARD DAWKINS has argued against such an upbringing, suggesting it "borders on cruelty" to present only one side of the debate concerning God's existence.

HUMANISTS disagree with people being taught in separate faith schools, and argue that people should look at the evidence (or lack of) for the claims of Christianity without being influenced to have to believe. Humanists argue that belief in God should not be forced upon a child when they are very vulnerable and likely to believe what their influential parents teach.

However, a child who has a religious upbringing can **REJECT** a **RELIGIOUS FAITH** for different reasons.

- **NEGATIVE EXPERIENCE** - They may have had a negative experience of the Christian community or become bored with attending church and feel they have had too much religious input into their lives.

- **DOUBT GOD'S EXISTENCE** - They may have never seen prayers answered, or never witnessed a religious experience, which has caused them to doubt God's existence.

- **MORE INTERESTING** - As the child develops, they may find other views more interesting because they are hearing them for the first time from friends or people at school who have not had a religious upbringing.

- **INDEPENDENCE** - It might be a statement of independence for a person who has had a religious upbringing to purposely choose not to follow that religion for themselves and reject arguments for the existence of God. Moreover, they may have looked at arguments against God and found them convincing.

NEED MORE HELP ON PHILOSOPHY OF RELIGION?

Use your phone to scan this QR code

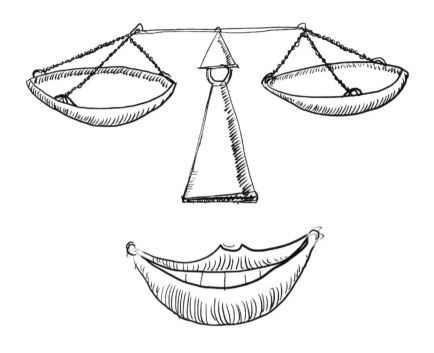

Equality

KEYWORDS

- **ABSOLUTE POVERTY** - A condition in which a person lacks the income to provide for their basic needs, such as food and water, sanitation and health

- **DISCRIMINATION** - The unjust treatment of people based on prejudice against their race, colour, nationality, age or sex

- **EQUALITY** - The state where people are treated fairly and equally, and no individual or group is favoured over another

- **HUMAN RIGHTS** - Rights which belong to every person regardless of status

- **PREJUDICE -** Having preformed opinions not based on experience

- **RACIAL HARMONY** - People of different races living and working together in peace

- **RELATIVE POVERTY** - The condition in which people lack the minimum amount of income required to maintain the average standard of living in the society in which they live

- **RELIGIOUS FREEDOM** - The right to choose to belong to a religion and practice its teachings without interference

- **SOCIAL JUSTICE** - The equal distribution of resources, opportunities and privileges to all people within a society

CHRISTIAN TEACHING ON HUMAN RIGHTS

Human rights are rights to which all people are entitled. The **UNIVERSAL DECLARATION OF HUMAN RIGHTS** was drawn up by representatives of over 50 members of the United Nations in 1948 to give people basic freedoms and rights, following the devastation of WWII. All people should have the rights to such things as freedom of expression, privacy, to seek refuge, to be treated equally by the law, to education and to not have to face torture. In 2015 the UN restated that:

"The Universal Declaration promises to all the economic, social, political, cultural and civic rights that underpin a life free from want and fear. They are not a reward for good behaviour. They are not country-specific, or particular to a certain era or social group. They are the inalienable entitlements of all people, at all time, and in all places - people of every colour, from every race and ethnic group; whether or not they are disabled;

citizens of migrants; no matter their sex, their class, their caste, their creed, their age or sexual orientation."

Christian teaching would support the view that all people should be given rights and freedoms, and treated with dignity and respect:

- **UNIVERSAL DIGNITY** - All people are "made in the image of God" (Genesis 1:27), which gives them a dignity not based on their status

- **NO FAVOURITISM** - Paul writes that, "God does not show favouritism" (Romans 2:11), and James writes that neither should we (James 2:1-4)

- **UNIVERSAL LOVE** - In the way that he lived Jesus showed that he had love for all people, and not just a special few. In the Parable of the **GOOD SAMARITAN**, Jesus taught that loving your neighbour means loving everyone, not just those we like or are in the same social group (Luke 10:25-37)

Sometimes, the most vulnerable groups in society are the ones that are not treated with dignity and given the rights they should have, so the Bible gives special attention to this. In Proverbs 14:31, a warning and instruction is given:

"He who oppresses the poor shows contempt for their Maker, but whoever is kind to the needy honours God."

The Christian Church has a lot in common with atheist and human respect for human rights.

- **WORKING TOGETHER** - Christians, humanists and atheists work together in the poorest areas of the world to ensure basic rights are respected

- **UNIVERSAL RIGHTS** - The protection of the right to freedom of expression, education and liberty are shared amongst Christians, humanists and atheists

However, Christian teaching, such as that given by Archbishop Rowan Williams in 2012, is that the reason rights are universal is because people are made in the image of God. He argued that if this moral and spiritual understanding of universal human rights is taken away, then they could become something simply imposed by authority. As humanists and atheists do not believe in God, then the basis for human rights between Christians, humanists and atheists is very different, even if the three groups can work towards trying to put them in place.

There are also divergent Christian responses to human rights. The Roman Catholic Church has expressed that whilst dignity must be given to people of all sexual orientations, the right to same-sex marriage is not a human right.

The Catholic understanding of marriage is:

> *"A matter of justice and fidelity to our Creator's original design. Redefining marriage furthers no one's rights, least of all those of children, who should not purposely be deprived of the right to be nurtured and loved by a mother and a father."*

The Roman Catholic Church and some Protestant Churches also argue that the right of a woman to become a priest is not a human right, as the Church priesthood being male is something ordained by God and not under the authority of the UN or any other secular body. The **DIVERGENT** Christian positions are normally due to the differences between secular and religious law, even if there is much agreement between religious and secular agencies on supporting human rights.

Within **SITUATION ETHICS** human rights are upheld if that is the most loving thing to do, which it normally is. However, this is assessed in each situation. A situation ethicist might decide that the most loving thing to do would be to extract information from a person who knows where a bomb is hidden. This might involve torture, which is not a loving thing to do to an individual, but is the most loving thing to do in order to save thousands of lives.

CHRISTIAN ATTITUDES TOWARDS EQUALITY

Because every person is made in the image of God, and Christ died for all, humans regard everyone as equal. This is further shown in teaching such as Galatians 3:26-29, which says that people's status in Christ is above their nationality or race: Paul writes that:

> *"There is neither Jew nor Greek, slave nor free, for you are all one in Christ Jesus"*

However, it is clear that there is inequality in many parts of the world, for a variety of reasons:

- **POOR LIVING CONDITIONS** - Caused by war, corruption, failed crops, economic mismanagement
- **INACCESSIBILITY** - To education, for example
- **DISCRIMINATION** - Different treatment of particular groups, such as women, ethnic minorities, the disabled

These inequalities impact upon the opportunities people have for their basic needs to be met, and to work, to learn and to flourish, physically, socially and economically.

Living the Christian life will involve challenging inequality and discrimination wherever it is found, and promoting the rights of all people to be treated fairly. Because Jesus taught Christians to love one another and demonstrate the love of God in the world, Christians try to overcome these inequalities by:

- **NATIONAL LOBBYING** - Working at a local and national level to represent those who suffer from inequality. Representations are made by different churches to government about the impact that policies will have upon disadvantaged groups. For example in a book entitled "On Rock or Sand? Firm Foundations for Britain's Future", the Church of England questioned whether everyone was benefiting from government policy, blaming welfare cuts and **POVERTY WAGES** for a rise in income inequality.

- **INTERNATIONAL LOBBYING** - International Christian organisations such as **WORLD VISION** focus on work to reduce global inequalities, organising programmes which concentrate on relief, development and advocacy. Following a report highlighting the inequality of health provision round the world, World Vision proposed practical ways in which the gap could be closed in its **CHILD HEALTH NOW** programme

CHRISTIAN ATTITUDES TOWARDS RELIGIOUS FREEDOM

Addressing a global conference of religious leaders in 2014, **POPE FRANCIS** said that religious freedom is:

"A fundamental right which reflects the highest human dignity, the ability to seek the truth and conform to it."

In previous teaching, Pope Francis said that people of different religions are not rivals or enemies, but brothers and sisters, and that when a person is secure in his or her own beliefs, "there is no need to impose or put pressure on others." This is confirmed in the official teaching of the Catholic Church. **CATECHISM** 1738 and 1747 talk of freedom in religious matters as an "inalienable requirement of the dignity of the human person" which must be protected.

The teaching of the Pope represents the views of many Christians who believe that there should be freedom for people to choose to follow different religions, and that education in UK schools should include teaching about a range of faiths.

This does not mean, however that all Christians believe that truth can be found in every religion.

There are different Christian views about the truth of the message of other religions:

- **EXCLUSIVE** - Christianity is the only true faith. In this exclusivist view, held by many Protestant and Evangelical Churches, as well as people within the Catholic Church, Christians should actively seek to spread the Christian faith and invite all non-Christians to convert.

- **DUTY TO CONVERT** - Other religions have partial truth, but only Christianity has the whole truth. Christians should encourage those of other faiths (and none) to convert. This view is held by the Roman Catholic Church and some Protestant Churches.

- **INCLUSIVE** - Some liberal Christians believe that Christianity is one of many faiths, all of which have some truths, as if they are different paths leading up the same mountain.

The Church often works together with other faiths to promote the welfare of the local community or national faith relations, for example in the Bradford Faith Forum, or in the **INTER FAITH NETWORK** for the UK. Such work can bring the benefits of getting to know other views, promoting harmony within society, learning about other cultural expressions, and Christians understanding their own faith better as they engage with others and hear different views about Christianity.

Living in a multi-faith society can also bring challenges such as people being questioned about their own views, which might lead them to struggle in their faith. Such a society can also expose tensions between different faith groups, and where truth claims clash this could cause disharmony in society.

In October 2016, The British Humanist Society addressed the issue of **RELIGIOUS FREEDOM**, stressing that this should not mean religious views should have more rights to be expressed than those that are non-religious. Quoting the European Convention on Human Rights, the BHS argues that everyone should have the right to freedom of thought, conscience and religion and suggests that the first two are often missed out when issues of freedom of expression and the rights of religions are quoted.

HUMANISTS and **ATHEISTS** have also objected to some Christian faith schools only presenting a very narrow perspective to students, as well as the giving of charity by Christian groups, such as Samaritan's Purse, that is accompanied by evangelical literature which aims for conversion of the person who receives the gift.

In response, Christian groups have argued that the faith is presented with no pressure to convert, and charity given is not dependant on the person following Christianity. Some Christians feel that they are being asked to keep their faith private, which goes against what the British Humanists would themselves argue, as they would support the **FREEDOM OF RELIGIOUS EXPRESSION**. Sharing the Christian faith is a vital part of how many Christians live, and which they feel the Bible encourages them to do, as long as it is done with gentleness and respect (1 Peter 3:15).

CHRISTIAN ATTITUDES TOWARDS PREJUDICE AND DISCRIMINATION

In the **PARABLE** of the **GOOD SAMARITAN** in Luke 10:25-37, Jesus tells a story about a Samaritan who acted with kindness and mercy towards a Jewish person. The Samaritans and Jews were hostile towards each other and had little interaction, and so the fact that the story records the Samaritan helping the Jewish person would have purposely shocked the listeners. Jesus tells the story to show that everyone is a neighbour and we should not practice prejudice and discrimination to any individuals or group.

PREJUDICE, which is holding preformed views of another person or group of people, often leads to discrimination, which acts unfairly against a particular person or group based on things such as gender, religion, age or sexual orientation. Prejudice and discrimination go against Christian teaching that states that everyone is made in the image of God, and the instruction to love one another.

Christians should not hold prejudice against other religions:

- **NO PREJUDICE** - In Acts 10 and 11, Peter's prejudice against the Gentiles (non-Jews) is challenged when he hears that God has no favourites

- **NO FAVOURITISM** - In Galatians 2:1-10, Paul says that external appearances do not matter as God does not show favouritism to any group

Prejudice and discrimination in society causes disharmony. It can lead to:

- **IMBALANCE** - The feeling that one group is less important than another

- **SOCIAL UNREST** - People do not feel they are valued and part of a society

- **HOSTILITY** - Between groups where one feels that the other gains privileges and opportunities that are denied to their own group

Suggestions that prejudice and discrimination is present in the UK include lack of equal representation:

- **INDUSTRY** - At the highest level of industry and business of women, ethnic minorities and people with disabilities

- **NON-CHRISTIANS** - Non-Christian religious and humanist viewpoints in the media

The UK government tries to address discrimination by passing laws that prevent discrimination based on grounds of gender, race, religion, sexual orientation or age, in areas such as employment.   It has also passed laws to make it an offence to stir up religious hatred.

Christians try to follow the example of Jesus in treating all people with equal respect. They work at a local level to try to challenge prejudice and encourage the equal treatment of all people. Ugandan born Archbishop of York, **JOHN SENTAMU**, has worked hard to tackle racism at both a local and national level, including publicly challenging the police for stopping and searching him 8 times during his time as Bishop of Stepney. He has also questioned the way in which prisoners are treated in Guantanamo Bay, a US detention camp occupied by suspected terrorists, most of whom are Muslims.

CHRISTIAN ATTITUDES TOWARDS RACIAL HARMONY

In **JOHN 13:34** Jesus said that people can show they are followers of his by loving others. This teaching, along with the belief that everyone is made in the image of God, informs Christian attitudes towards people of different races, and encourages them to work for racial harmony. If God does not have favourites, then Christians should not favour one group over another.

This teaching is emphasised in all Christian Churches:

- **CHURCH OF ENGLAND** - George Carey, the former Archbishop of Canterbury said that:

  "Racism has no part in the Christian Gospel. It contradicts our Lord's command to love our neighbours as ourselves. It offends the fundamental Christian belief that every person is made in the image of God and is equally precious."

- **ROMAN CATHOLIC CHURCH** - In the Second Vatican Council (1962-1965), said that:

  "Discrimination on grounds of sex, race, colour, sexual conditions, language or religion is incompatible with God's design."

Archbishop **DESMOND TUTU** worked to bring an end to racial segregation in South Africa. Black people were not allowed as many rights as white people under a system called **APARTHEID**, and Tutu used speeches, sermons, non-violent protests and calls on government to end a system that was against Christian values and beliefs. Although he suffered several times for his faith, he was able to see the end to Apartheid in 1994. Motivated by his faith, Tutu said that God's dream was that people lived together as family; Tutu commented that if it wasn't for his faith he would have given up his struggle to bring equality. He noted that the Bible speaks of a God who:

"Turns you around to be concerned for your neighbour. He does not tolerate a relationship with him that excludes your neighbour."

Within a society where races and people from different ethnic backgrounds live together:

- **LEARNING** - People can learn from each other

- **UNDERSTANDING** - Have their understanding of the world expanded

- **CHALLENGING** - Have racial and ethnic stereotypes challenged

- **DIFFERENCES** - Understand their own background better as they explain it to others

- **EXPRESSION** - Enjoy the benefits of different ethnic expressions, such as food, clothing, music and dance, and ideas about family

Within **SITUATION ETHICS**, acting in the most loving way would suggest that racism would not be allowed, as it does not show love for another human being. However, Joseph Fletcher, the person who originated the theory, was keen to say that people have the freedom to make their own moral decisions in a situation, as long as that decision follows the law of love. **BISHOP ROBINSON**, who originally supported this theory, abandoned it as he thought that this individualist approach would lead to moral chaos. Under Situation Ethics, people can reject any rule in a particular situation, including those against prejudice and discrimination, which means that racial equality might not be respected if it is felt that the most loving thing is to overrule it.

CHRISTIAN ATTITUDES TOWARDS RACIAL DISCRIMINATION

Because Christians support racial harmony, they are against, and work to end, racial discrimination. Through the Parable of the Good Samaritan, and the way in which he shocked his followers by speaking to a Samaritan woman (John 4), Jesus taught his followers that to discriminate against people because of racial, or any other, differences was wrong. In other parts of the New Testament, this message is repeated. For example, in Acts 17:26, Paul teaches that:

"From one man God made every nation of men, that they should inhabit the whole earth."

In further sections, Peter is taught that he should not think that there are special privileges for certain races, realising that God has given the same gift to different people who believed in Jesus. He came to the conclusion that he would be opposing God if he continued to think that other groups of people were inferior (Acts 11:17).

Racial discrimination can cause problems in society:

- **NOT VALUED** - It can make certain races feel that they are not valued in society by discriminating against them in terms of employment or housing opportunities

- **ANGER** - It can cause social unrest and anger

- **UNWELCOME** - It can make people feel unwelcome and unable to progress in society

- **LACK OF REPRESENTATION** - It can lead to lack of representation of people from certain racial backgrounds in important and influential fields such as at the top level of business, finance, police and government. Without being represented in these fields, people can feel that their voice is not heard and that they do not belong to a society where such discrimination occurs.

Christian leaders such as Desmond Tutu and Martin Luther King have opposed racial discrimination as against Christian teaching. Churches Together has spoken out against racism and its effects on society by saying that:

"Respect for the humanity we share with each and every neighbour is the only one basis for a peaceful and good society. Any attack on the dignity and human rights of any racial or religious group damages all of us."

CHRISTIAN ATTITUDES TO SOCIAL JUSTICE

Christians believe that anything that makes it impossible for a person to flourish is against the Bible's teaching that Jesus came to enable people to live life to the full (John 10:10). But in many parts of the world and in the UK, people do not have equal access to economic opportunities, employment, education, health care and even the facilities for their basic needs to be met.

Reasons People Suffer a Lack of Social Justice

▸ Distribution of Wealth

A small percentage of people earn vast amounts of money and many millions of people struggle to survive:

- According to inequality.org the 8% of people who own over $100,000 of assets in total (including property, car etc) own 87% of global wealth

- The 0.3% of people who own between $1 million and $30 million own over 12.8% of total global wealth

- The United States and Canada has 10% of the world's population but 75% of the world's income

- The bottom half of the global population own less than 1% of total wealth

▸ Housing

People cannot afford their own home, and live in unsuitable rented accommodation, which can cause ill health

▸ Employment

People cannot find work as they do not have the qualifications or have access to education or training to enable them to find employment; this can affect different groups more than others. In 2015 the UK unemployment rate for young black people aged 16-24 was 27.5% compared to 13.1% for white people and 24.3% for people of Asian ethnic background.

Solutions to a Lack of Social Justice

Christians believe that they should show God's love for other people by getting involved in the world, and trying to make social justice more possible for those who suffer.

The Salvation Army, a Christian Church and charity, try to help people who struggle to have access to opportunities. They do this by:

- **TRAINING** - Offering training to help people find employment

- **SHELTER** - Helping people with emergency accommodation and teaching living skills so that a person or family will be able to cope in society and access the opportunities offered in society

- **FOOD BANKS** - Running food banks so that families can be fed and have enough income to pay bills etc

- **LOBBYING** - Working with other agencies to present concerns and issues to government so that it is aware of the reality of social injustice

- **LOANS** - Organising short term loans such as The Mustard Seed project in developing countries, which enables a family to start up a business

Christians are motivated by the teaching of the Bible, which encourages people to look out for the needs of those who suffer social injustice:

- **MATTHEW 25:31-46** - Jesus teaches that those who visit prisoners, clothe the naked and feed the hungry will be rewarded in the Kingdom of God.

- **ISAIAH 58:6-7** - God says that true service involves breaking the chains of injustice, setting the oppressed free, feeding the hungry, providing shelter and clothing the naked.

- **AMOS 5:12** - God is angry against those who deprive the poor of justice in the courts. Those who love God should "speak up for those who cannot speak for themselves, for the rights of all who are destitute." They should "defend the rights of the poor and needy." (Proverbs 31:8-9)

In other ways, many Christians respond by giving financially to charities that help to fight injustice and pray for the needy.

Situation Ethics Responses

- **LACK OF LOVE** - People who are suffering social injustice are obviously not being shown love, which contradicts the ethical principle that is the basis of the theory. Joseph Fletcher believed that "justice is love distributed", which means that the injustices we see in the world are due to the lack of love.

- **FLETCHER** - He believed that any response to an ethical dilemma must be practical and relevant to each individual situation; but finding out what to do in a situation is not helped by the question, "what does the law say" but "who needs to be helped?"

- **END JUSTIFIES THE MEANS** - To enable people to know social justice Fletcher could allow for a law to be broken in a certain situation, as long as love was the overriding motive. The end justifies the means in situation ethics.

CHRISTIAN ATTITUDES TO WEALTH AND POVERTY

There are many reasons why poverty exists in the UK:

- **UNEMPLOYMENT** - Or poorly paid work

- **HOMELESSNESS** - Making a person dependent on the generosity of others and making it hard to find work

- **ADDICTION** - For example, drugs, alcohol, gambling, etc, which all costs money and makes it difficult to find work and housing; poor handling of income

- **LACK OF EDUCATION** - And/or a poor family situation which is difficult to break

In addition to the above, **GLOBAL POVERTY** exists because of:

- **UNEQUAL DISTRIBUTION** - Mismanagement and unequal distribution of resources, possibly including corruption, by a country's government.

- **WAR AND SOCIAL UNREST** - Which means that food supplies have been cut, or money used on funding the war rather than basic supplies.

- **ENVIRONMENT** - Climate change and adverse weather conditions which affect food supply and income

- **NATURAL DISASTERS**

These conditions, in addition to other factors such as greed and tyranny, can result in people living in absolute poverty. This is where a person or family do not have enough income to afford to meet their basic needs, such as food and water, medicine, sanitation and shelter. Absolute poverty can lead to malnutrition, untreated diseases and death, and is normally found in developing countries.

Relative poverty is the situation in which people lack the minimum amount of income required to maintain the average standard of living in the society in which they live. Although relative poverty might not result in death, it can often mean poor health and housing and shortened life expectancy. Relative poverty can be found in all countries.

Christian responses to wealth and poverty

On different occasions in the Gospels, Jesus instructs his disciples to give to the poor. Throughout the Bible, Christians are instructed to be generous and help the needy:

- **DEUTERONOMY 15:11** - "Be open-handed towards the poor and needy in your land"

- **JAMES 2:15-16** - "Suppose a brother or sister is without clothes and daily food. If one of you says to him, 'Go, I wish you well; keep warm and well fed,' but does nothing about his physical needs, what good is it?"

- **PROVERBS 14:21** - "Blessed is the one who is kind to the needy."

- **MATTHEW 25:35-6** - Jesus says that when people serve the poor and needy it is as if they are actually serving him

Although the Bible does not condemn wealth, it teaches on different occasions that it is difficult not to be consumed by it, and even more difficult for a rich person to keep God as a priority:

- **HAGGAI 1:3-4** - God says to wealthy people, "you eat, but never have enough; you drink, but never have your fill."

- **MATTHEW 6:24** - On different occasions, God warns that it is difficult not to be tempted by the pull of getting more and more money and warns that a person "cannot serve God and money" as they will be devoted to one and hate the other.

- **1 TIMOTHY 6:10** - Warns that "the love of money is the root of evil" and Jesus tells a parable about a man who built bigger and bigger barns, and paid no attention to God. In the parable, the man suddenly dies, and Jesus says, "this is how it will be with anyone who stores up things for himself but is not rich towards God."

■ **MARK 10:17-27** - Jesus is asked by a rich man what he must do to enter the Kingdom of God. Jesus replies that he must sell all he has and give it to the poor. The man failed this test, which showed that his priority was money not God. After telling the story, Jesus said that it is hard for a rich man to enter the kingdom of God because of the power that money and wealth holds over a person.

Putting these teachings into practice, the organisation **CHRISTIANS AGAINST POVERTY** tries to meet people's needs in the same way in which Jesus did, with love, compassion and practical help. This includes offering free debt advice, help with budgeting, bills, mortgage and rent arrears and the control of spending, and running job clubs which help people find employment.

In the ethical theory **VIRTUE ETHICS**, which builds on the teaching of Aristotle, emphasis is given to the development of a person's character. The theory stresses that in living an ethical life, a person should do so out of the goodness of their nature and not just because they are obeying a set of rules laid down. This is similar to the teaching given above, as Christians believe that giving to the poor should be a joyful thing which comes from the heart, and that "God loves a cheerful giver" (2 Corinthians 9:7). Although coming at things from different angles, Virtue Ethics and Christianity would agree that giving to the poor must be genuine and the outward act of giving should match the inner moral attitude, as Jesus teaches in Matthew 6:1-2.

NEED MORE HELP ON EQUALITY?

Use your phone to scan this QR code

Exam Success

Exam Preparation

Answering the Questions

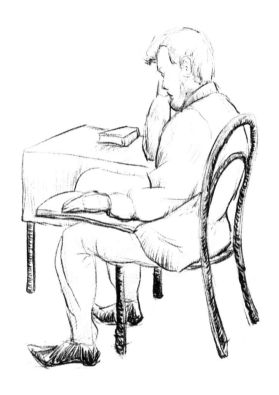

Exam Preparation

HOW THE EXAM IS STRUCTURED

In the Edexcel GCSE Religious Studies Full Course, you will take **TWO EXAMINATIONS**, which are each **1 HOUR & 45 MINUTES** in length. One examination will cover Christianity and the other will examine a second faith from a choice of Islam, Judaism, Buddhism, Sikhism or Hinduism.

The Christianity examination will cover one Area of Study from the three in this revision guide. The second examination will cover a different Area of Study from the one examined for Christianity, studied from the perspective of another religion.

▸ Example no. 1

You study Christianity Area of Study 1 and Islam for Area of Study 2 (see separate revision guide for Islam). Each Area of Study is examined in a separate paper of 1 hour 45 minutes. The only combination that isn't allowed is to study Christianity for one Area of Study and Catholic Christianity for the other Area of Studerretwqy.

▸ Example no. 2

You study Islam for Area of Study 1 and Christianity for Area of Study 3. Each Area of Study is examined in a separate paper of 1 hour 45 minutes

In each examination, there are **FOUR QUESTIONS** to answer. These questions relate to the 4 sections of the Area of Study you have chosen. So, for example, if Area of Study 1 is chosen, you will answer one question on Christian Beliefs, one on Marriage and the Family, one on Living the Christian Life and one on Matters of Life and Death.

Each of the 4 questions is split into 4 parts: A, B, C and D

▸ **Part A** - 3 marks

▸ **Part B** - 4 marks

▸ **Part C** - 5 marks

▸ **Part D** - 15 marks*

In Sections 1 and 3 (Christian Beliefs and Living the Christian Life), part D is worth 15. In the other two sections, Marriage and Family Life and Matters of Life and Death, part D is worth 12 marks. This is because 3 extra marks are added in the first and third section for the quality of written communication. In the exam, these questions will be shown with an asterisk (*) and it will be clearly outlined to you that these questions carry more marks than the other part D questions. The total marks available on each paper is 102.

How you are marked

▸ **Questions A, B and C** - 50%

The first three questions on each section assess your knowledge and understanding of the religion and belief. This is a total of 50% of your marks.

▸ **Question D - 50%**

The last questions on each section assesses how you analyse and evaluate religion and belief. This is a total of 50% of your marks.

This means that you do not have to give your **PERSONAL OPINION** or viewpoint in parts A, B and C, but are expected to in part D.

HOW TO BE SUCCESSFUL

There a number of things you can do to prepare well for the exam. This next section outlines the key skills that you need to master, and advice on how to answer the different types of question. There are further resources available on the website.

Analyse the specification

Edexcel cannot ask you anything that is not on the specification

So, there will be no nasty surprises in the exam. Take the time to know the content of the Area of Study you have been taught.

This book and supporting website are organised according to the structure of the specification, so this should help you in developing your notes and planning your revision.

Develop a revision system that works for you

- **REVISE EQUALLY** - The four sections in the Area of Study you have been taught receive equal numbers of marks, so you should give equal amount of time to studying them

- **DON'T LEAVE TO THE LAST MINUTE** - Don't leave revision of the four sections until before the exam. Revise each section as you are taught it, creating revision material each week

- **PRODUCE SUMMARIES** - Of the four sections as you go along

Prepare thoroughly for the exam

- **TRY SAMPLE QUESTIONS** - Throughout the year, have a go at sample exam questions on each of the four sections

- **KNOW YOUR TIMINGS** - This exam is 105 minutes long, and there are 102 marks available - about a mark per minute. Towards the end of each section, go through exam questions under timed conditions, as this will help you know how long you should be spending on each question in the exam.

Learn the technical language

You need to know and be able to use technical, or specific, religious language. You will use this language in every type of question in the exam, so developing your knowledge and understanding of these words is essential:

- **KEYWORDS** - Learn the language as you go along using the keywords at the beginning of each section; understand the definition of these words so that you can use them in the different parts of the exam

- **USE OFTEN** - Use this language at every opportunity - in class discussion and in written work.

- **USE THIS BOOK** - Learn the **KEY CONCEPTS** and **COMMAND WORDS** at the end of this section

- **UNDERSTAND THE DEFINITIONS** - Make sure you know what each Command Word means so that you are sure you know what the question is asking you to do. This is explained below.

Show that you know a variety of sources of wisdom and authority

- **PART C** - You will always be asked to refer to a source of wisdom and authority

- **PART D** - You will be asked to refer to Christian teachings

- **SHOW YOUR KNOWLEDGE** - Use teaching from the Bible or the Catechism of the Catholic Church or the 39 Articles to give depth to your explanation of different Christian beliefs. Look back through the sections of this revision guide where sources of authority and wisdom and Bible verses are always in bold.

Be clear which religious groups you are dealing with

- **USE THE RIGHT LANGUAGE** - To speak about a particular group, for example, Catholics or Protestant Christians, rather than making sweeping statements. This will improve the quality of your answers

- **RECOGNISE & EXPLAIN** - Show the differences between groups; in part D you will be asked to refer to different Christian teachings

- **USE EXAMPLES** - To explain beliefs and show that you know how a particular teaching works in practice. This course is called Beliefs in Action

Clearly show how beliefs, teachings and attitudes guide behaviour

When answering questions that ask you to explain or evaluate, it is important to be able to refer to how beliefs, teachings and attitudes can lead people to behave in particular ways:

- Teachings inform beliefs

- Beliefs influence attitudes

- Attitudes affect behaviours

Practice how to answer questions in the right way

▸ **Outline or State** - part A questions

- State three facts without explanation (see below for examples)

- Do not give your personal opinion or develop your answers

▸ **Explain or Describe** - parts B and C questions

- Develop the idea you are presenting

- Illustrate your answer with examples and details of the point you are making

- Question B and C can ask you to explain a Christian view or views, which means you will need to provide reasons behind the view/s.

- Do not give your personal opinion, but show why the Christian belief or beliefs you have explained or described is/are important

- Part C will require you to refer to sources of wisdom and authority to explain religious points of view

▸ **Evaluate** - part D questions

   ■ **JUDGE** - Whether a statement is good/true/right/wrong in your view

   ■ **CONSIDER** - Different opinions on the issue and weigh up the evidence on the different sides

   ■ **REFER AND EVALUATE** - Different Christian teachings and non-religious views, as well as ethical and philosophical arguments. Read the question carefully for what views are required

   ■ **JUSTIFY** - Your reasoning and conclusions

KEY CONCEPTS

The following key concepts apply across the specification. Make sure you learn, understand and use them:

GOD	**SUFFERING**	**AUTHORITY**
REVELATION	**THE FALL**	**WISDOM**
BIBLE	**EVIL**	**INCARNATION**
JESUS	**FORGIVENESS**	**TRINITY**
THE HOLY SPIRIT	**BELIEF**	**HUMANISM**
HEAVEN	**RECONCILIATION**	**ATHEISM**
HELL	**JUSTICE**	**SITUATION ETHICS**
SALVATION	**PRAYER**	**SANCTITY OF LIFE**
ATONEMENT	**UTILITARIANISM**	**EQUALITY**
RESURRECTION	**CATECHISM**	**OLD/NEW TESTAMENT**

NEED MORE HELP ON EXAM PREPARATION?

Use your phone to scan this QR code

The Exam Factory

Answering the Questions

PART A QUESTIONS - 3 marks

Command words: State or Outline

Part A questions will ask you to **STATE THREE** or **OUTLINE THREE** features or beliefs, or activities. For example:

▸ **STATE three Christian beliefs about marriage**

Or

▸ **OUTLINE three examples of crime**

Or

▸ **OUTLINE three activities a Christian might do on a pilgrimage**

Part A questions test **FACTUAL KNOWLEDGE** and **UNDERSTANDING**, and are worth 3 marks, one for each of the things that you state. You will be marked using **ASSESSMENT OBJECTIVE 1** (AO1), which tests knowledge and understanding of religion and belief.

- You will need to be accurate and correct in what you state, but do not need to develop your answer

- This is a place in the examination where you may be able to pick up some time, as long as you are precise, and state or outline 3 distinct features

- You can write these 3 things separately in the space provided in the exam paper, or write them as one paragraph, as long as there are 3 features given

PART B QUESTIONS - 4 marks

Command words: Explain or Describe

Part B questions will ask you to **EXPLAIN TWO** or **DESCRIBE TWO** types or theories or beliefs or reasons or teaching. For example:

▸ **DESCRIBE two theories of punishment**

   Or

▸ **EXPLAIN two different Christian beliefs about abortion**

   Or

▸ **DESCRIBE two types of Christian worship**

Part B questions are short answer questions that test your **FACTUAL KNOWLEDGE** and **UNDERSTANDING**, and are worth 4 marks, two for each of the things that you describe or explain. You will be marked using AO1.

- It is important that you realise the difference between part A and part B questions.

- Explaining or describing is different to stating, and requires you to develop both of the points you make in more detail.

- You can develop each point you make by giving an example of what you mean.

- You can also refer to different groups within Christianity who have different beliefs.

- Use technical language - the first example question given above could include words such as deterrence and restoration, with a description of each. The second example could use terms such as the sanctity of life and the quality of life as they are relevant to Christian beliefs about abortion.

- Do not waste time giving your personal opinion, as this is not needed.

- Make it easier for the examiner to see the points you are making by writing them separately in the space provided in the exam paper.

- Make sure that when a part B question asks you to describe or explain two different beliefs, these are two different beliefs and not the same belief explained in two different ways.

PART C Questions - 5 marks
Command words: Explain

PART C questions will ask you to **EXPLAIN TWO** reasons or ways in which a Christian would respond. However, There is an **EXTRA MARK** available for a **PART C** question, as you are required to include a **SOURCE OF WISDOM** and **AUTHORITY**, such as the Bible, or Catholic teaching etc. For example:

▸ **EXPLAIN two reasons why working for justice is important to Christians. In your answer you must refer to a source of wisdom and authority.**

Or

▸ **EXPLAIN two different beliefs about divorce in Christianity. In your answer you must refer to a source of wisdom and authority.**

Or

▸ **EXPLAIN two ways in which Christians respond to the problem of evil and suffering. In your answer you must refer to a source of wisdom and authority.**

Part C questions test your **FACTUAL KNOWLEDGE** and **UNDERSTANDING**, and are worth 5 marks, two for each of the things that you explain and one for a reference to or quotation from the Bible or teaching of the Church or another source of wisdom and authority. You will be marked using AO1.

- One of your answers has to be supported by a source of wisdom and authority. This source can be a direct quote of a Bible verse or Church teaching, or give the Bible reference after the point you have made. For example, Christians think all people are made in the image of God (Genesis 1:27)

- Show the examiner how the source of wisdom and authority supports and develops the point you are making, or informs the Christian belief you are explaining. See sample answer below for how to do this

- It is important that you note the difference between part B and part C questions

- Explaining or describing is different to stating, and requires you to develop both of the points you make in more detail

- You can develop each point you make by giving an example of what you mean

- You can refer to different groups within Christianity who have different beliefs

- Use technical language. The first example question given above could include sources such as, "treat others as you wish to be treated" as a reason why Christians believe they should work for justice. The second example could use terms such as natural and moral evil

- Do not waste time giving your personal opinion, as this is not needed

- Make it easier for the examiner to see the points you are making by writing them separately in the space provided in the exam paper

- Make sure that when a part C question asks you to describe or explain two different beliefs, these are two different beliefs and not the same belief explained in two different ways. If you are not sure which group of Christians believe a particular thing, say "some Christians believe that … "

PART D QUESTIONS: 12 marks

Command words: Explain

Part D questions will ask you to **EVALUATE A STATEMENT** and consider arguments for and against it. You will need to weigh up different opinions and give your own considered view. In each part D question, you must:

- Refer to Christian teachings

and then:

- Different Christian views

- And/or non-religious views

- Give a justified conclusion

The question will give clear instructions about what views you are required to refer to, and part D also should include relevant reference to the ethical or philosophical arguments studied in the Area of Study.

For example:

▸ "Christians should be against euthanasia" (12 marks)

EVALUATE this statement considering arguments for and against. In your response you should:

- Refer to Christian teaching

- Refer to different Christian points of view

- Refer to non-religious points of view

- Reach a justified conclusion

In this question, 3 of the marks awarded will be for your spelling, punctuation and grammar and your use of specialist terminology.

‣ **"Jesus had to die" (15 marks)**

EVALUATE this statement considering arguments for and against. In your response you should:

- Refer to Christian teaching

- Refer to different Christian points of view

- Reach a justified conclusion

‣ **"It is impossible to have a just war" (12 marks)**

EVALUATE this statement considering arguments for and against. In your response you should:

- Refer to Christian teaching

- Refer to different Christian points of view

- Reach a justified conclusion

Part D questions test how well you can **ANALYSE** and **EVALUATE** opinions, views and beliefs, and are worth 12 marks, or 15 in sections 1 and 3, where marks for written communication are also awarded. You will be marked using **ASSESSMENT OBJECTIVE 2**, which tests the ability to "analyse and evaluate aspects of religion and belief, including their significance and influence."

- Your answer must come to a considered conclusion. It will not gain many marks if it just lists a range of views. Explain the reasons that support your viewpoint and how your view relates to the different views you have studied. You are allowed to agree with or link your opinion to a viewpoint you have presented, but must explain why you agree, and why you disagree with other views. Explain your views in full sentences and paragraphs, not bullet points.

- You can only gain half the marks if you do not refer to different viewpoints

- Read the question very carefully to see what the different views are that you are required to refer to in your answer. Use the bullet points in the question to help you structure your answer, and try to be very logical in how you lay out your answer in part D.

- You must refer to Christian teaching from sources of authority and wisdom. Show the examiner how the source of wisdom and authority supports and develops the point you are making, or informs the Christian belief you are explaining. See sample answer for how to do this.

- The different viewpoints you give must be developed and explained, before you evaluate them.

- Use connecting words between your paragraphs, such as "in contrast" or, "alternatively", or, "however". These make your answer have a sense of flow, which is good in an extended response.

- You can develop each point you make by giving an example of what you mean, and by using the word because … eg, Christians believe this because, as it will lead you to give reasons Christians/humanists/atheists etc. have for certain viewpoints.

- Use technical language. The first example question given above could include terms such as, "the sanctity of life" and "the quality of life". You can then evaluate the different points of view that use these concepts. The second example could use terms such as "The Fall", "sin", "forgiveness", "redemption" and "atonement".

- Make it easier for the examiner to see the points you are making by writing them separately in the space provided in the exam paper

- You should prepare for every part D question by knowing different Christian viewpoints on each of the sections

EXEMPLAR

Area of Study 1

▸ **Part A) Outline three activities a Christian might do on a pilgrimage (3 marks)**

Basic response

Pray, worship and walk to a special site.

Developed response

During a pilgrimage a Christian will PRAY to get closer to God, WORSHIP as part of the community of pilgrims, and WALK in silent meditation TO A SPECIAL or sacred SITE which has a particular meaning in Christianity.

The additional explanation shows that the student has good knowledge of the three activities they have named, and how they are part of a pilgrimage. The extended answer is still only one sentence long

▸ **Part B) Explain two ways Christians respond to the problem of evil and suffering (4 marks)**

Basic response

Christians will respond to the problem of evil and suffering by praying, and carrying out charity work.

Developed response

Christians will respond to the problem of evil and suffering by praying that God will relieve the suffering of those affected by natural evil and help those who are trying to bring aid, because they believe God is omnibenevolent and concerned about those in need.

In addition, another way in which Christians, like those in The Salvation Army, will respond is to carry

out charity work because they believe that they should show God's love and kindness to others, and this is a practical way of doing that.

The developed response shows that the student has good knowledge of the two Christian responses, giving some explanation about them. In the first sentence of the developed response, technical terms such as prayer, natural evil and omnibenevolent are mentioned, and an example is given of two things Christians would pray for. In the second sentence, introduced with a connecting phrase, a distinct second response is explained and a Christian group is mentioned.

▸ Part C) Explain two reasons why the incarnation is important to Christians. In your answer you must refer to a source of wisdom and authority (5 marks)

Basic response

The incarnation is important to Christians as God became a human and lived on earth in order to restore His relationship with humanity. Secondly, the incarnation is important because it shows that God understands what human existence is like, as the Bible says.

Developed response

The incarnation is important to Christians as God became a human and lived on earth in order to restore His relationship with humanity. This means that, if they want to, humans can know God through Jesus. The Bible says that "God loved the world so much that he sent his One and Only Son" so that humans and God could connect again.

Secondly, the incarnation is important because it shows that God understands what human existence is like. This means that God knows the full experience of what it is like to feel pain, joy, hunger and other human experiences, and this helps Christians feel that God knows what they are going through.

Look carefully at the developed response. There is clear understanding about why the incarnation is important to Christians, which is what the question asks you to show. The reasons why it is important are given some development and both sections refer to a source of authority and wisdom. The phrase, "humans and God could connect again", is not the best, but an attempt to explain a restored relationship, which is the point being made in paragraph 1. Now look again at the difference between the basic and the developed responses.

▶ ***Part D) In this question, 3 of the marks awarded will be for your spelling, punctuation and grammar and your use of specialist terminology.**

"A Christian should believe the world was made in seven days." Evaluate this statement considering arguments for and against. In your response you should:

- Refer to Christian teachings

- Refer to different Christian points of view

- Reach a justified conclusion (15)

Basic response

Some Christians believe that the Bible is <u>literaly</u> true. If the Bible says that the world was made in seven days, then that is what happened. There is no need to question that, and no one was there apart from God so <u>sceintists</u> have no idea really. This is what Christians who <u>literaly</u> believe the Bible think and it is not right to doubt God if God said it in Genesis.

Some other Christians, like <u>Cathlics</u> believe in the Pope. The Pope said that the Bible is not <u>literaly</u> true, and the world could have taken a long time to be created. The Big Bang theory was made by a <u>Cathlic</u>. God started the Big Bang and this has more evidence than the Bible's story of how the world was made.

I don't think the world was made in seven days because the Bible is an old book and no one really believes it. Science is more reliable.

You can see why this is a low or very basic level of response:

- Two different Christian viewpoints are given, but they are very basic, and the second one does not explain a Catholic view

- The answer refers to Genesis, but gives no detail or reference, and why it is important

- The second paragraph gets a bit side-tracked. The Big Bang theory is not explained, and no reason is given as to why it is there. There isn't really a logical flow to the answer

- There is a lack of technical terms and quite a few spelling errors

- The conclusion does not really have any justification - the Bible being an "old book that no one believes" is not a justification but an **ASSERTION**, which means a statement without support. The student needs to show why science is more reliable to make this a justified conclusion.

Developed response

When answering a part D question, it is useful to have a template, so that you stay focused on the question. A template can help you, in the pressure of the exam, to maintain a logical flow.

Here is one that could help you, using the word **E.A.S.Y**. as an acronym. (Be aware, that RS GCSE is not easy, but this is an "easy" word to remember in an exam). Easy stands for:

- **EXPLAIN** what Christianity, or a group within Christianity believes, using technical terms

- **ADD** a Christian teaching and source of authority and wisdom which supports and informs that belief, and an example to develop this point

- **SUGGEST** an alternative view, which might be your own or another Christian group, or that of an atheist or humanist, or reference to an ethical theory such as Situation Ethics. This depends what the question asks for. Add an example here too

- **YOU** now give a considered evaluation of these views, and your conclusion, giving justified reasons for your view/s. Make a direct reference to the question

So, using this acronym, your answer to the above question about the creation of the world in seven days might look like this:

Some Christians, called Creationists, believe that the Bible should be taken literally. The Bible is God's word telling humanity what happened at the beginning of the world, and is a reliable account because the author is God. Creationists believe that the Bible outlines how "God created the heavens and the earth" and what happened on each of the first seven days of creation. It outlines how land and sea, plant, animal and human life all happened within that time. Young earth creationists believe the world is roughly 10,000 years old and was formed by God over seven literal days because the Bible records that as the time it took.

A Christian view has been **EXPLAINED**, using technical terms. Reference to teaching is given (God created the heavens and the earth), with an example of land and sea etc. used to back this up. A reason for this view is **ADDED** - the Bible, as a source of wisdom and authority, is a reliable account, because it is God's word and God is the author. The last sentence gives reference to a very specific belief from young earth creationists.

In contrast, other Christians believe that the story in Genesis is not meant to be taken literally but metaphorically. It still says important things such as God being the creator of all life, but we should not take the seven day description literally. This is the belief of many Roman Catholic Christians, including Pope Francis, who think that some parts of the Bible are meant to be read literally, like historical accounts of battles, but not every part, like the Genesis creation story. Francis argues that this does not change the fact that God is the creator but enables a person to read the Bible in the correct way.

Notice that the paragraph starts with a connecting phrase, "in contrast". This helps give the answer a sense of flow. An alternative Christian view is **SUGGESTED**, and explained, using technical terms such as metaphorical. A reason for this view is given - the Bible is not to be read literally in every part. The last sentence gives reference to the Pope and Catholic teaching as a **SOURCE OF WISDOM AND AUTHORITY**.

Furthermore, many Catholics, who also do not believe the Genesis story of seven days should be taken literally, have helped to research scientific understandings of the creation of the world. Priest and scientist George Lemaitre proposed a theory that later became known as the Big Bang Theory. This suggested that the world is formed over billions of years, not created in seven days, and the Catholic Church now accepts this in its teaching.

This paragraph develops the second one, and shows this connection by the use of the word "furthermore". It goes into detail about an alternative explanation to a seven day creation of the world, without going away from the question. It **SUGGESTS** further alternatives to the viewpoint explained in the first paragraph, and gives a specific **EXAMPLE** (the Big Bang Theory) to support this alternative view, and says that this view is accepted and supported by a **SOURCE OF AUTHORITY**, the Catholic Church.

On balance, there seems to be a lot more evidence for the second view, as the science supports the Big Bang Theory. Like the Pope said, I think Christians can still get a lot of meaning from the story in Genesis without believing that the story has to be literally true. So, the statement is wrong, as a Christian should not have to believe that the world was made in seven days.

The Bible says that "The Earth is the Lord's and everything in it" (Psalm 24:1) and I think that Christians can still believe God created the world, but over a longer period of time, as the scientific evidence suggests and many Christians who are also scientists, such as Rev. Professor John Polkinghorne, support.

This paragraph offers a **JUSTIFIED CONCLUSION**, as it suggests why the evidence is stronger on one side of the debate than the other.   It shows that it has **CONSIDERED DIFFERENT CHRISTIAN VIEWS**, and also **MAKES A DIRECT REFERENCE TO THE QUESTION**. It refers to other **SOURCE OF WISDOM AND AUTHORITY**, such as the Bible and a Christian scientist.

EASY!!

It is perfectly possible to get high or full marks in this exam, with careful preparation and making sure that you know what the question is asking you and how to answer it.

NEED MORE HELP ON ANSWERING THE QUESTIONS?

Use your phone to scan this QR code

Lightning Source UK Ltd.
Milton Keynes UK
UKOW04f1835130217

294314UK00002B/48/P